About the Author

Celeste Donohue was born and raised in Philadelphia, where she started her performing career at the age of twelve. By the time she was twenty-three, she was on her way to Los Angeles, where she worked as a dancer, singer, actor, and comedian. But it was writing that always came the easiest. Initially writing for magazines, that led to copywriting, blogging, and scriptwriting. After many years of rewriting her resume, she finally got around to writing her first book about all the day jobs she's endured while pursuing a career in entertainment.

Hollywood Factotum

Celeste Donohue

Hollywood Factotum

Pegasus

PEGASUS PAPERBACK

© Copyright 2025
Celeste Donohue

The right of Celeste Donohue to be identified as author of this work has been asserted by her in accordance with the Copyright, Designs and Patents Act 1988

All Rights Reserved

No reproduction, copy or transmission of this publication
may be made without written permission.
No paragraph of this publication may be reproduced,
copied or transmitted save with the written permission of the publisher, or in accordance with the provisions
of the Copyright Act 1956 (as amended).

This book is a memoir. It reflects the author's present recollections of experiences over time. Some names and characteristics have been changed, some events have been compressed, and some dialogue has been recreated.

Any person who does any unauthorised act in relation to this publication may be liable to criminal prosecution and civil claims for damage.

A CIP catalogue record for this title is available from the British Library

ISBN-978-1-80468-103-9

*Pegasus is an imprint of
Pegasus Elliot MacKenzie Publishers Ltd.*
www.pegasuspublishers.com

First Published in 2025

**Pegasus
Sheraton House Castle Park
Cambridge CB3 0AX England**

Dedication

This book is dedicated to the people who follow their dreams. And the people who hate their jobs.

Acknowledgments

I want to gratefully thank Jim Martyka, without whose help this book might still be sitting on my desktop. I'd like to acknowledge the bad bosses I've had, who, without their terrible management and people skills, I might never have written this book. I want to thank the teachers I had along the way who believed in me and the teachers who taught me how to change my life. Lastly, I want to give a giant thank you to my family and friends for their endless support.

"Perhaps someday I'll crawl back home, beaten, defeated. But not as long as I can make stories out of my heartbreak, beauty out of sorrow" – Sylvia Plath

"Remember your dream is your only scheme, so keep on pushin'" – Curtis Mayfield

INTRODUCTION

Over the years, I learned very much the hard way that we truly do create our own circumstances, good and bad, and now I am able to look back on these times and see all the mistakes I made. It took me many years of struggle and forty-nine jobs in Los Angeles to figure this out.

This compilation is about what I had to do to make money and survive so I could pursue a career in entertainment in Hollywood. The irony is that I wanted a career in entertainment to avoid having jobs I didn't like or want, and in pursuit of my dream, I've had nothing but jobs I didn't like or want. These are the stories about those jobs: the people, the experiences, the quittings, the firings, the celebrity encounters, the men I hooked up with, the memories, and the hard-learned lessons.

I'm happy to share these stories, and I'm hoping I can help others avoid some of the same mistakes. I also hope to help people become more aware of their *mindset* because mindset and attitude go a long way and have a big influence in your life, whether you're aware of it or not.

I've studied and learned a tremendous amount about our subconscious mind. One thing I've learned is that no matter what you might think about yourself on a conscious level, there are so many deep-rooted beliefs and programming that we are acting out of most of the time without even knowing it. Learning about this changed my life!

At the very least, I hope my story entertains you because I believe *everyone* has a story to tell. The reason I chose to tell this one is because I don't know anyone who's had as many jobs as I have. I'm sure there are people out there who have, but maybe they haven't written a book about it.

Also, I hope this book inspires people to know their rights in the workplace because so many employers take advantage of those who don't know. I hope it urges people to leave soul-sucking jobs they hate because life really is too short. I also hope it inspires people not to give up on their dreams no matter how hard things get. It's easy to give up, and it's definitely *not* easy to keep going, but it's worth it.

A couple of final notes: some of the names of the businesses and/or the people the people I worked with have been changed, mainly so that I don't get sued, but many have not. Also, I did my best to keep things in the order they happened over thirty-three years, but there were a lot of overlaps and working more than one job at a time, so I'm not completely sure everything is in the exact proper order, but it's as close as I could get.

Like I said, and like you'll see, there were a lot!

PREFACE: HOLLYWOOD HERE I COME!

fac·to·tum – /fak'tōdəm/
noun
1. an employee who does all kinds of work.

Before I get into the jobs, I need to give you just a little context.

This tale of survival starts in 1990 when I proclaimed to my mother that I wanted to move to California to be a performer. Her response was, "Take your brother and sister with you." I was twenty-three years old and the third of four children, three of whom were still living at home. My mom clearly wanted an empty nest, so shortly thereafter it was decided that myself, two of my siblings, Kris and John, and my good friend Pat would make the trek across the country from Upper Darby, Pennsylvania, to Hollywood, California!

I had asked several of my friends to make the move with us, but in the end, Pat was the only one who took the offer. The four of us left on a hot day, June 10, 1990, to be exact. About a week before we left, I bought a little Ford Ranger pickup truck with a stick shift and no air conditioner (big mistake) so that we had more room for our belongings, which wasn't much. The four of us packed up in the Ranger and my sister's Toyota Tercel and got ready to move west.

Since we didn't have cell phones, we bought walkie-talkies to communicate as we drove across the country. I remember on the day we were leaving, feeling a mixture of sadness—knowing I would miss my mom, dad, and oldest sister—but also excitement to finally start my life. I don't know about my fellow travelers, but I was ready for this journey with $1,200, my clothes, and some black-and-white headshots that we got somewhere in downtown Philly a few weeks before. I was totally prepared!

Back in 1990, I must say I was ripe for Hollywood. I was a good age, had long blonde hair, was in good shape from my years of dancing, with a broad smile. I've always had a toothy smile, but not in an overly toothy, Julia Roberts kind of way. I didn't think I was beautiful, but I thought I was attractive enough. Around that time, my friend Jeff described me as a girl "who looks like a California blonde on the outside but is like Wednesday Addams on the inside."

Speaking of Wednesday Addams, when I headed for Hollywood, aside from my clothes, I left all of my other belongings back in the funeral home that I grew up in, but that's a story for another book because that's a whole different *undertaking* than this story…

After high school, I bounced around doing odd jobs for a while and at the same time trying to figure out what to do with my life. I hated school and didn't want to go to college, hence the one year I spent in community college in art classes, much to my dad's chagrin. Once I got hired as a dance teacher, things became clearer. I loved teaching and considered opening up my own dance studio, but I knew teaching wasn't enough for me. I wanted to be a performer! I wanted to be a star!

You see, with three other siblings and dead bodies in the basement, I had a lot of competition for attention, so it was always something I craved. I knew as a kid that I was never going to get that attention at home, so I looked elsewhere, and performing was the remedy. I started as a cheerleader, but then I joined the school band, and that's when I was "bitten by the bug," as they say. I didn't know in high school that I would eventually move to Hollywood, but I was starting to realize I didn't want a "regular" life. I didn't want to do what I saw many other people doing—including my dad—which was working a job you didn't like just to pay your bills and/or support your family.

Also, once I saw the movie *Fame*, I was inspired! I started going to dance classes, and the more I danced, the more I wanted to perform. So much so that I performed a solo to the theme from *Shaft* in my high school talent show. This probably wasn't a smart idea, because I wasn't really good yet, but I did it anyway because I was never the type of person who would let fear stop me. I also love to take risks, which will become more obvious as we move through this story. That seems to be my nature.

Prior to moving to L.A., my performing experience consisted of four years in my grade school band, where I played the flute and performed a solo of "The Hustle" in eighth grade, and ten years of dance training (four years teaching), which included many solos in the annual recital. Between that and my recently acquired bartending school certificate, I was ready to take on Hollywood. At this point in my life—you know, when you're young and delusional—I believed I had enough experience and was willing to work hard. I figured that was enough to take me where I wanted to go. Very naïve of me in retrospect.

My brother John's good friend, Jamie Kennedy (yeah, *that* Jamie Kennedy), had moved to L.A., the year before with a few of their friends from our neighborhood. They told us we could crash at their place when we got to L.A. so at least we had a place to land, and from there we would figure out where to live.

After taking pictures and saying our goodbyes to the family, we took our two-car caravan south to Virginia, as Roanoke was our first overnight stop. After that, we moved on to Georgia, where we stayed with a guy named Mike, who I had met the previous year in London. He was in the army, and we stayed in touch over that year with actual handwritten letters, and when I let him know about our journey, he offered for us to stay with him in Augusta. Before we left, he gifted me with a "fuzz buster," a little device that detects when cops are around. It was appreciated by all of us, and we used it the rest of the trip.

We left Georgia, drove through Alabama and Mississippi, and our next stop was New Orleans! I sang for the very first time in public at a karaoke bar, and this planted the seed for my singing career, which would start several years later. From New Orleans, we drove through Texas, which is ridiculously tiresome. We stayed in San

Antonio for one night, and then, for some stupid reason, we stayed in El Paso for two nights. El Paso isn't somewhere you want to be for two hours, much less two nights, but there we were at the ratty hotel pool getting fried by the Southwest summer sun, which none of us had experienced before.

We stopped at the Grand Canyon, and this is one time when I will use the word "awesome" to describe something. I think that word gets used out of context too much, like when people say things like "these mozzarella sticks are awesome." But the Grand Canyon is truly an awesome sight.

That last day of driving seemed the longest because I was beside myself with excitement to get to Hollywood. We were actually staying in North Hollywood with Jamie and friends, but this was a couple of years before Jamie made a name for himself. Also, there is a big difference between Hollywood and North Hollywood. The latter is in the San Fernando Valley, the porn capital of the world, but aside from that fun fact, the Valley is hotter and less interesting, and back then, North Hollywood was still kind of sketchy. It has since become a hip little area, that's if you consider the Valley hip, which I never did and still don't.

We arrived at our friends' apartment in the afternoon, and everyone seemed to be excited that we were there, all of us from Upper Darby and now hanging out and drinking beers in Los Angeles together. It was an unforgettable time, at least for me. There were seven or eight of us sleeping in this apartment, which had one bedroom and a small loft upstairs that was used as a bedroom. One of us was on the couch, and a couple on the floor. We knew that we couldn't stay in this situation and immediately started looking for our own apartment. Instead of looking in the Valley, we went right "over the hill" into Hollywood and started looking for "For Rent" signs and bought a copy of the *Los Angeles Times*. Remember when you used to look for things in a newspaper, like jobs and apartments?

We came across a two-bedroom, two-bathroom apartment in the heart of Hollywood on Argyle Avenue, right above Franklin Avenue, at the foot of the Hollywood Hills. A man named Santos was the landlord. He seemed to take a liking to us when we told him we had just driven across country, and were new to Hollywood, so he agreed to rent to us. I can't say I remember if he ran a credit check, and none of us had jobs yet, so he really took a chance on us.

It was a new, peach-colored building at the top of the street that was riddled with drug dealers and users at the bottom of the street. We lived on the third floor with the apartment facing the noisy courtyard. None of us had beds, just clothes, some blankets, a boom box, and one futon cushion that my sister and I slept on in the master bedroom while the guys slept on the floor in the other bedroom. Each bedroom had a bathroom but no common area bathroom, which was strange, and there was a little living room with the small kitchen connected as part of the same room. I don't know what drunk architect came up with this odd floor plan, but we were just happy to have our own floor to sleep on. We decided in order to conserve our funds we would wait and buy beds until after we got jobs.

Here we were, living in Hollywood, where we could see Capitol Records from our apartment. We were just two blocks away from Hollywood Boulevard! My dreams were officially about to come true … or so I thought. First, I had to find a way to support myself.

JOB #1: THE CREPE PLACE ~ COUNTER PERSON/CASHIER

Before I tell you about my first job, it would be remiss of me to leave out this detail after being in Hollywood for a very short time. Within the first few days, myself, and my fellow journeymen had to do some touristy things too, so we bought a map to the stars' homes, which in L.A. is a popular thing to do for tourists. In retrospect, it's actually a very weird thing to do.

As we were driving down Rodeo Drive in Beverly Hills, I noticed that Gene Kelly's house was on this street. As a dancer, he was one of my idols because he truly was one of the greats, and so handsome too. At this time in 1990, he was a fairly old man but a living legend, so when I saw him walking down the street, I about lost my mind. My sister was driving, and I suddenly exclaimed, "There he is! It's Gene Kelly! Pull over!"

I jumped out of the car and convinced my brother to come with me as I chased Gene Kelly down the street until I caught up with him. He was with his wife, who was clearly a lot younger than him, and she could have been invisible as far as I was concerned. I started blathering on to him about how I was a dancer from Philadelphia and what a big fan I was and just making an overall idiot of myself until he put his hands up in an "okay, I've heard enough" manner. He wasn't appreciative. He was annoyed if anything, and I suddenly felt completely dejected.

I disappointedly slithered away and walked back to the car, confused as to why he wouldn't want to hear from such a big fan. Of course, later I understood why he would have this reaction to being accosted by some stranger while out for a stroll with his wife. That's why famous people live in L.A., so that this kind of thing won't happen. That's how I learned not to approach or act like celebrities are a big deal. And maybe it isn't the ideal story of meeting one of your idols, but I can still say I met and got brushed off by Gene Kelly!

As for the job, these were the days before the internet, so you had to apply for jobs in person. No one had a resume back then, at least not for the kind of jobs we were looking for like bartending and waiting jobs. While driving down Santa Monica Boulevard through West Hollywood, with stars in my eyes, I somehow spotted a "Help Wanted" sign on the window of a crepe shop, not far from the famous Troubadour club, which helped launch a number of music acts in the Sixties and Seventies.

It wasn't a restaurant, more like a donut shop that sold crepes instead of donuts. I went in and filled out an application, and I'm proud to say I was the first one to land a job, even if it was working the crepe counter as a cashier. I can't remember the name because it was over thirty years ago and it's not there anymore, but back then it was located on the corner of Santa Monica Boulevard and Almont in West Hollywood. West Hollywood was the first place I had ever been to where there were gay bars out in the open. It wasn't quite as flamboyant as it is today, but the old landmark bars like the Mother Lode, Micky's, and Rage were always busy and fun. There was so much liberation and openness in L.A., and so far, I was loving everything about it!

Quick side note about the product I was selling: I've never understood the enthusiasm over crepes. They're not pancakes, they're not tortillas, so what are they? Just a thin piece of weird, flimsy French batter.

I showed up the next day and was trained on taking orders and working the cash register, which wasn't difficult, having already been both a waitress and a cashier (before L.A.). It turns out that smiling *was* difficult for me. In fact, after one day of training, I was fired because I wasn't smiling enough at the customers. It wasn't a very busy place, so I *didn't* smile at that many people, but the point is, I didn't even get a chance to hate that job, which I'm sure I would have, considering I found nothing to smile about. I'm not sure what their expectations were or exactly how miserable I looked to have gotten fired after only one day, but this was an indication of what was to come. I had no idea that getting fired would become as chronic for me as Dr. Dre's ground-breaking record.

JOB #2: THE RAINBOW BAR & GRILL ~ COCKTAIL WAITRESS

After I got fired from the crepe place, I was on the hunt again. While roaming up and down Sunset Boulevard, I stopped at The Rainbow in West Hollywood. If you haven't seen the documentary *The Rainbow* about this legendary place, I highly recommend it because it has an interesting history. Originally, the restaurant was the Villa Nova restaurant, which was owned by film director Vincente Minnelli who was married to Judy Garland at the time and the father of Liza. Joe DiMaggio and Marilyn Monroe met at the Villa Nova on a blind date in 1952. After being in business for twenty-eight years, the Villa Nova closed in 1968 and re-opened as the Windjammer for a few years until it closed in 1971.

In April 1972, it reopened again, this time as The Rainbow, a rock club, with a party for Elton John. After that, it became a regular hangout for the likes of John Lennon, Ringo Starr, Jim Morrison, Keith Moon, Alice Cooper…the list goes on and on. Apparently, John Belushi ate his last meal of lentil soup at The Rainbow. When the Eighties rolled around, it started to change into more of a heavy metal crowd (not my scene) and bands like Motley Crue and Guns N' Roses were regulars, along with Lemmy from Motorhead, who lived close by and was a usual fixture at the bar.

I didn't know any of this amazing history when I stopped in during the middle of a hot summer day in 1990 to apply for a job. If you've never been to the Rainbow, the décor is worth mentioning. The first floor is covered in red tables that are surrounded by red booths, which are perfect for rock n' roll stars to cozy up together and snort lines off the tables. There was a fireplace in the main room, which always made it feel warm on those cold, January L.A. evenings of sixty degrees. There is a small bar in a separate room with a few stools where people would be four deep trying to order drinks, and nothing about the interior looks like it has been updated in years, or ever. But the food was good.

The day I went in, the owner, Mario Maglieri, was there with his slicked-back hair. After filling out the application, he hired me on the spot. I didn't realize at the time how landing a gig at a place like this was very coveted, and I can only assume that I got hired because of my youth and looks: two of the most valuable commodities in Hollywood. I was to show up the next night ready to be a cocktail waitress. I had waitressing experience from Philly, so that wasn't the problem. No, the problem was what I was wearing because when I showed up the next night, he told me I needed "dress sexier." I followed someone around that night for training and learned the ins and outs of cocktail waitressing at The Rainbow.

I came back to work the next night in a slightly sexier outfit, complete with shorts, a tank top, and cowboy boots. I now cringe at the thought of both the request and the outfit. That seemed to satisfy him. Now I was on my own and ready to work.

The real problem was the crowd.

I was put upstairs in the bar area, entitled "Over the Rainbow," not downstairs in the restaurant, and I don't know if that would have made a difference. They packed in these rocker dudes and chicks like sardines. I remember hearing from someone that a lot of clubs in L.A. would pay the fire department so they could break the crowd code. Whether they did or not, I'm not sure, but it was awful, and half of the drinks landed on my shirt from people bumping into me. Trying to collect money and give change was all but impossible. I walked by Tommy Lee in my booze-soaked t-shirt that night, and he smiled, but I was too angry to smile back.

I walked up to the manager in the middle of the shift of my second night and told him that I had to leave immediately because my brother was in a car accident. I don't know why I didn't just say "this isn't for me" and leave. Instead, I told an extreme lie, which seems ridiculous now, but that's the kind of stupid thing you do at twenty-three years old. Also, this was before cell phones, so I'm not exactly sure how I would have gotten the message that my brother was in an accident, but it wasn't the first time I used someone dying to get out of something. I have grandparents who have died several times.

So that was my brief employment at the legendary Rainbow. Maybe if I had known that getting a job at such a famous place was an opportunity other girls would've killed for, I would have stuck it out, but I doubt it. I didn't think it was worth it. I've been there several times since; it hasn't changed, and it's considered an L.A. landmark, so I feel proud to say I worked and quit there. It's a much more fun place to be as a customer than an employee, at least from my experience.

JOB #3: THE WHITE PELICAN ~ WAITRESS

I finally found a job that lasted more than two days, and I had to go all the way to Santa Monica to get it. I was living in Hollywood, so making the fifteen-mile, forty-minute commute to Santa Monica for a waitressing job was not ideal, but doing it back in 1990 was a hell of a lot easier than it is now because the traffic gets worse every year. I was also getting desperate, having already lost two jobs in a matter of days.

The job was on Main Street at a cute, little restaurant called The White Pelican (it's now a Mexican restaurant called Lula's). It was a bright, open, beachy kind of place with big windows in the front and a patio in the back. Some things I found interesting upon being a new arrival and waitress in L.A. were that people here liked ordering egg whites only for breakfast, and they also loved something called "ceviche," which I found to be disgusting once I knew what it was. Raw fish? So gross! It's funny when you grow up in a certain place and some things that seem so normal now were so foreign to me when I first got here. I had heard of sushi, but ceviche was a new and nasty way to prepare raw fish that I was learning about.

During the first few weeks in L.A., the four of us went to a restaurant called "The Source" that was on Sunset and Sweetzer. It's an abandoned spot right now. We didn't know when we went in that it was a vegetarian restaurant, and for four kids from Philly, who grew up on cheese steaks and hoagies, vegetarianism wasn't even in our consciousness. We looked at the menu, looked at each other and asked each other questions like, "What the hell is brown rice, and why is it brown?"

What I remember most about The White Pelican (besides the weirdos that ordered ceviche) were a few of the celebrities that came in. Most importantly, Bruce Springsteen. When I was growing up, my whole neighborhood loved "The Boss," maybe because he is known as the voice of the blue collar, which was definitely my neighborhood. He just seemed like such a cool guy, which I found to be true as I took his breakfast order with shaking hands. I wanted to get an autograph so much, but that is just something you don't do...as I learned from my Gene Kelly experience. And when you're waiting tables in L.A., you have to act like celebrities are everyday people, but this was Bruce! I didn't want to get fired, so I kept myself under control and just smiled a lot at him.

Another minor celebrity that I waited on was Robert Hegyes, aka Juan Epstein from *Welcome Back, Kotter.* Back in 1975, while all the girls were swooning over the young John Travolta, I was into the short Puerto Rican (who wasn't Puerto Rican in real life). I'm not sure why I liked him either, but was sad to learn he died in 2012, especially when he was such a nice customer twenty-two years prior.

I also was introduced to my first L.A. boyfriend in this restaurant. My friend Pete, from Philly, had come to visit and had been in the Navy with Steve (the eventual boyfriend), who lived in Long Beach. Steve came to the restaurant to meet Pete while I was working, and we were introduced. We hit it off and started a fun but tumultuous relationship that went on for a while before Steve moved to Colorado in 1992. We went out long enough for Steve to bail my brother out of jail after his car got impounded and to have a wild adventure in Tijuana, Mexico, that included a bloody lip after drunkenly falling off a stage in some bar and then scaling a fence in the rain to get to our seedy hotel. I guess I felt this was worth mentioning because it was after Steve that I started dating people I worked with almost exclusively. He was the exception to what was to become almost a rule for me.

Not much more to tell about this job other than this was my first experience with a Mexican kitchen staff. If you don't live in L.A., you might not know that at least ninety-five percent of all kitchen staff in Los Angeles is Mexican—no matter what the food is. So, with that said, anyone who's against immigration should dine in Los Angeles before you get so disgruntled about it. I've noticed the people who get the most indignant about immigration are the ones least affected by it.

Also, if you want to learn to speak Spanish, work in an L.A. restaurant, and you'll at least pick up the basics. And if you want to learn a good work ethic, model yourself after the Mexican immigrants as, at least in my experience, they tend to be very hard workers.

I worked here for about four months. I know I left this job because I was only working breakfast and lunch shifts, and it was too far a drive for the amount of money I was making. I also left this job because I got the next job on the list, but "The Pelican," as we called it, was the start of my L.A. restaurant career that went on and off for several years.

Unfortunately.

JOB #4: GORKY'S RUSSIAN BREWERY ~ MANAGER

I got this job while my sister and brother were still living here in late 1990. I remember because the movie *The Doors* was coming out and there was heavy promotion for it. A lot of billboards around Hollywood, the Doors' music playing everywhere, and it felt like we were back in the Sixties. It had such a fun hippie vibe, and I loved it!

There were two locations of Gorky's Russian Brewery: Hollywood and downtown L.A. The downtown restaurant opened first in 1981 and was named after Russian playwright Maxim Gorky. I think it's important to mention that at this time, there was *nothing* in downtown L.A. except the Jewelry District, some artists on the fringe, and Gorky's. No one went downtown because there was no reason to go there, but that changed drastically once they built the subway line and (what was then) the Staples Center. Now downtown is thriving with overly expensive new apartment buildings, restaurants, and a huge homeless population.

Gorky's slogan was *"Foodski, funski, brewski"* and it was a unique-ski place. It was cafeteria style that served an odd mix of dishes, including omelets and chili to stuffed cabbage and borscht soup. They also brewed their own beer in visible giant tanks, which was a novelty back before brew pubs became a popular thing. There were large wooden booths, and paintings from local artists covered the walls. The Hollywood location, on Cahuenga Boulevard half a block up from Hollywood Boulevard, naturally attracted actors and other hipster types, but the downtown location, at 8th and San Julian St. and on the edge of skid row, had been popular among the artist community and anyone else brave enough to live downtown at the time. Both locations had live music on the weekends and were open twenty-four hours a day because who doesn't want a bowl of borscht at three a.m.?

Both of my siblings were now working at the Hollywood location, and my sister was a manager there. She recommended me when they were hiring for a manager at the downtown location, which was kind of a bummer because I lived in Hollywood. I wanted to work in Hollywood because I knew some of the people who worked there and had a crush on the now famous actor, Kyle Chandler, who briefly worked there as a bartender. But honestly, the original downtown location was cooler than Hollywood. That is, aside from the rats in the basement, which I refused to go into, and the owner, who allegedly had a coke problem. Both of which might have had something to do with Gorky's going out of business in 1993. I remember hearing someone say, "He snorted that restaurant up his nose," but that could have just been a rumor.

This was another short-lived gig, and thankfully the rats and landing my next job forced me to move on, which was a good thing because aside from when I was sitting at the end of the bar sipping free beer and eating free food, I didn't like being a restaurant manager. It's long hours, low pay, and constant problem-solving. But it's too bad Gorky's isn't around anymore because it really was a different kind of place that stood out among all the places in L.A. that try so hard to be hip. It *was* hip, it was fun, and I'm glad I got to experience it.

But I still think borscht should never be on any menu in any restaurant.

JOB #5: UNIVERSAL STUDIOS ~ DANCER/MOUSE

While still working a restaurant job, I found out in *Drama-Logue*, the then go-to publication for non-union auditions, that Universal Studios theme park was holding dance auditions for a new show that was going up. It's important to note my mindset at this time. I was still within my first few months of being in L.A., and I was full of hope and excitement. Anything was possible! In retrospect, my mindset had everything to do with getting this job, which was my first real entertainment job. As time went on, my mindset changed, but I'll get to that a little later.

The show was *An American Tail—Fievel Goes West*, based on the Steven Spielberg-directed animated kid's movie of the same name, about a family of mice that move from Minsk to Utah. I never understood why Utah was the destination; it's not like they were Mormon mice. If anything, I always assumed they were Jewish mice since their last name was Mouskowitz.

The auditions were at the Debbie Reynolds Dance Studio in North Hollywood, and I loved this dance studio. There were several rooms for various types of classes, rehearsals, and auditions. One had a grand piano in it, and the hallways were decorated with posters of Debbie Reynolds movies and headshots of many celebrities who took classes or rehearsed there, like Michael Jackson, among others. One side note, the studio was demolished in 2019. Very sad because I went to many classes and auditions there, so I have lots of good memories.

The audition consisted of fairly simple dance routines, and at the time, I didn't know why they were so simple. I had no idea what I was getting into as far as the costume was concerned, but I was thrilled to land the job.

I was cast as "Mama Mouse," the mother of Fievel, who was the star of the show and probably about six in mouse years. To this day, I still have never seen the movie. The show was about twenty minutes long, and we all danced around in giant mouse costumes to the choreography that we spent several weeks learning. Aside from wearing those hot costumes in the L.A. summer heat, it was an easy gig. Hence, the simple dance routines. My vision was out of the mouth of the giant mouse head, and I wore a heavy bodysuit with an attached hoop skirt. It was a great way to stay in shape, especially doing five to seven shows a day.

There were three teams of performers: the red team (which I was on), the white team, and the blue team (the backup team). Naturally, because we were in our twenties and made up of mostly performers, drama often ensued in the trailer that we were holed up in in between shows. It was a small space for ten performers plus the puppeteers who handled the giant, mechanical cat. Just for space, sometimes between shows some of us would tan ourselves outside of the trailer because when you're in your twenties, who cares about skin cancer or heat stroke? Dancers would get into arguments, cry, and storm out. It was like a little soap opera taking place within a theme park. Personality conflicts, competition, and all kinds of dramatic moments always kept it interesting.

For example, Susan, one of the girls who played Fievel's sister in the show, told me and my friend David (who played Papa Mouse) a story about a trip she had made to a water park. She said when she went down this big slide in the water park, she hit the water so hard that her bathing suit gave her a wedgie bad enough that it made her ass bleed. We laughed, but she assured us that it wasn't funny, and it was really painful. We tried to be understanding and empathetic, and she told us not to tell anyone. We immediately told our friend Larry, another mouse. He didn't say much, but later, in between shows, several of us were watching a Tom Cruise movie. Larry was sitting on the couch reading the paper while Susan (the bleeding ass victim) and other cast members were gathered around the TV. Since Larry wasn't watching the movie, I said, "Larry, don't you like Tom Cruise?"

Without missing a beat, he said, "Tom Cruise makes my ass bleed." Susan shrieked and turned to look at David and me, who were trying not to laugh but couldn't hold it in. Furious, she got up and stormed out of the trailer, slamming the door. She didn't talk to us for days.

In addition to the trailer drama, we would often have to do "meet and greets" after the show, and the kids would flock to Fievel but would give some of the other characters attention if Fievel was too swarmed. One of the characters was named "Gussie," and on the red team, this character was played by Fred, a Black man (his identical twin brother played the same character but on the white team). During a meet and greet, Gussie bent down to shake one of the kid's hands. The kid looked directly into Gussie's mouth (the vision hole) and was able to see Fred. He suddenly yelled out, "Gussie ate a Black man!" It's hilarious how kids' brains work.

One of the funniest memories I have involves Fievel's head coming off during the show. As you might expect, kids and their parents were the majority of the audience, and the kids loved Fievel. All the girls who played Fievel had to be short, roughly five feet tall. When wearing the costume, Fievel's face was at their chest, and the girl's head stuck up over his face but was covered by Fievel's hat where the vision hole was. They had very little mobility with their upper body because their upper arms were also part of Fievel's head.

Halfway through the show, Fievel would run backstage behind a roll-up curtain, have a little costume change, and emerge in a cowboy outfit to make it clear that they were now "out West." Once he was in his new outfit, he would position himself behind the curtain, and it would roll up again to reveal the new cowboy, Fievel.

On this particular day, a girl named Alicia was playing Fievel. She was behind the curtain and ran out before the curtain was completely up and it knocked Fievel's cowboy hat off, but she was running so fast that she made it to the front of the stage before she could stop herself or realize her hat was off. There was Fievel's face with a human head sticking out of the top of it! Kids started screaming, and the parents looked horrified. Naturally, all the dancers started laughing, and Alicia panicked and ran off stage. We kept going as though nothing was wrong while they reattached the hat backstage, even though the soundtrack had Fievel speaking but no Fievel on stage. Eventually, Fievel came back out with the hat reattached and finished the show, but who knows how many kids were traumatized that day?

I know I was traumatized by working in a theme park. The crowds, the kids, the tourists with their cameras, and I still haven't been to or have no desire to go to Disneyland because of working at Universal. Two things I don't like: long lines and screaming children.

Some of the other live shows that were in the park at the same time were *Beetlejuice*, the *Wild West Show*, and *Miami Vice*, and everyone dated each other from different shows. I went out with one of the stunt guys from *Miami Vice* and one of the singers who played Dracula in *Beetlejuice*. In fact, the singer and I did our rendition of the classic "If This World Were Mine" at the wedding of one of my friends, the sister of the lead singer of 4 Non Blondes and the now-famous music producer, Linda Perry. I'm happy to say she gave us a standing ovation after we finished the song, but she was the only one. Everyone else just sat and clapped.

Other great memories from the Universal days were the rooftop parties my brother and I had at the end of the summer season. We were living in an apartment on Franklin Avenue that had a great rooftop space with chairs and lighting, so all we had to do was bring my giant speakers upstairs, set up a keg of beer, tell everyone to bring some food, and it was on! Everyone we worked with from Universal came to those parties. Also, during these early days, my brother and I, along with some other

American Tail cast members, played featured extras in a parade scene in the film *Jingle All the Way,* which was a Universal film.

Sadly, they eventually closed the show because periodically they replace the shows with more updated ones, but I had a great time working at Universal over the four years I was there, and I met friends that I still have to this day. Being there was where I first started to feel at home in L.A. because I was surrounded by other performers and like-minded people. One of my favorite things about Los Angeles is all the creative people who come to this city to pursue their dreams. There is a freedom of expression that I think is unique to this city, which I love and always will.

Working at Universal was also my introduction to unemployment. Since it was a seasonal show, we were eligible for unemployment during the months that we weren't performing. Little did I know that over the years, I would have the unemployment phone number committed to memory.

JOB #6: THE CRUSH BAR ~ BARTENDER

During the off-season at Universal, I needed extra money, so I had to pick up another job, and I was lucky enough to score a job as a bartender at The Crush Bar. I still remember what I wore to the interview, and I thought I looked cute.

I was very wrong.

It basically looked like a lime green maternity mini-dress with a black button at the top. I wore black crisscross lace-up shoes that matched the button. Somehow, they hired me anyway. I also want to address my fashion choices in the very early nineties. Always thinking I was fashionable, I arrived in L.A. and quickly learned that the acid-washed skinny jeans that I wore with black cowboy boots looked somewhat dated in the ever-trendy Los Angeles. I quickly took note and started to work on creating an updated look for myself. Luckily, there were plenty of stores on Hollywood Boulevard back then to help me with this.

The Crush Bar was located half a block above Hollywood Boulevard on Cahuenga Boulevard and was open on Thursday, Friday, and Saturday nights only. In those three nights, we made a killing!

It was owned by two brothers from Lebanon who oozed sleaziness. They wore polyester suits, gold chains, heavy and unpleasant cologne…everyone knows the type. But the draw of the place was definitely not the owners but the music. The DJs only played Motown hits, disco, and other music from the sixties and seventies. It had a line every night they were open, and even though the place looked like it hadn't been decorated since 1960, people loved it. The walls and thin carpet on parts of the floor were a dark red color. There were three bars with two bartenders working each. We served beer in cans only, and all the alcohol was served in plastic cups. No décor, no fancy Hollywood atmosphere, just a big dance floor and great music. What more do you need? The DJ booth was on a riser against the wall of the dance floor, and part of the wall was mirrored, which made the dance floor look bigger. The only seating was a few tables and chairs scattered around the perimeter of the room, so with very little seating, it encouraged people to either dance or just be wallflowers. But the music was too fun to not dance.

Celebrities came in once in a while. I remember serving Morgan Freeman and Samuel Jackson on the same night as they were guests of whoever was having their birthday party there. Another time I served Sharon Stone a drink and she gave me a friendly but condescending "thank you."

This place is still talked about. When I had my blog, entitled *Death to Hollywood,* which featured stories about growing up in a funeral home and my Hollywood experiences, I had an entry where I wrote about The Crush Bar. It was the post with the most comments by far, including former customers, employees, DJs, and bouncers, all sharing their thoughts and memories.

It was definitely the best bartending job I've had because I got to listen to the kind of music I liked all night long while slinging drinks and making a lot of money. Not a bad gig in my twenties. Not to mention all the hookups. During my part-time employment there, which was about two years, I made out with a bouncer, one of the DJs, a fellow bartender, and a customer. Another DJ asked me if I wanted to have a threesome with him and his wife, which I declined.

I also met a couple of musicians there who used to come in a lot, who I became friends with, and we hung out socially together. I was really into this very talented keyboard player who eventually went on to play for Janet Jackson and Mariah Carey, among many others. We had a couple of fun, brief escapades, and I got free tickets to a Janet Jackson concert. All jobs have their perks!

Once, after a particularly long night of partying with these musicians—the same night I passed O.J. Simpson walking out of Bar One—I woke up with a very bad hangover. When I was finally able to go out and get food, my friend David and I went down to a Subway that used to be right off the corner of the iconic intersection of Hollywood Boulevard and Vine Street. I ordered my sandwich and mentioned that I was hungover, to which the Subway "sandwich artist" suggested I drink Clamato. Do you know what's in Clamato? Clam juice. He no sooner said that, that I ran outside and puked into the gutter like some homeless junkie. My brother loves to remind me that seeing me puking on the corner of Hollywood and Vine is burned into some tourist's memory of Hollywood.

But the memory that sticks out most from the Crush Bar is the proposition I got from one of the owners. After I had been working there for a while, he told me he had a "business proposition" for me. I thought, *Maybe he'll make me bar manager, and I can earn more money.* I was very wrong! He told me he'd pay my rent if I had sex with him once a week. I was disgusted. My rent at the time was only $450 a month, so it wasn't exactly worth it, *and* he was married with a couple of kids. I gracefully declined by telling him I had a boyfriend, which I didn't since I was obviously making out with half of Hollywood, but I didn't want to lose my job by telling him how gross he was. I totally could've sued for sexual harassment, but when you're young, and long before the #MeToo movement, getting hit on by bosses was just part of the gig. It was, unfortunately, expected.

Meanwhile, another relative of the owners, whom I often worked at the same bar with, would regularly steal money. I wasn't going to rat him out, so I would just turn a blind eye because I wasn't about to get in the middle of family drama. He was doing drugs, eventually got caught, and around the same time, business was slowing down. L.A. clubs have a shelf life, and this club had a good run considering that it was around long before I got there. But after a few years, I wasn't making the money I was before and needed to move on. I left on weird terms because after I rejected the owner, he wasn't as nice to me as he had been before, and when I told him I needed to work full-time and make more money, he told me not to come back. After a few more years of dwindling crowds, they closed their doors only to reopen as a new club about a year later. Since then, there have been several clubs and restaurants in that space, but none of them ever saw the success of the legendary Crush Bar.

I don't have a lot of regrets in my life, but there is one regret that sticks out in my mind to this day.

One night, way back in 1991 or so, while working at the Crush Bar, I was at the Coconut Teaser, a club on Sunset Boulevard that used to be very popular. I was on the dance floor movin' and groovin' to the club music of the day. After several songs, I took a break to go to the bar and was approached by a woman who told me she liked the way I danced. I was flattered and thanked her for saying so. Then she said in so many words that she was looking for dancers for *Soul Train*, a TV show I had loved since I was a kid (I thought it was better than *American Bandstand*). Naturally, I was excited. I asked her what I would be doing and she said I would just be one of the regular background dancers you see on every episode. It wasn't a paying gig, but potential camera time. She gave me her card and told me to be at a certain address at 9am on Saturday morning.

I woke up early on Saturday morning and got ready to go to the studio in Hollywood where they produced the show. As I pulled up to the address, I saw a line around the corner of young adults like myself, and I realized they were there for the same reason. I drove around to see how long the line was, and it was wrapped all the way around to the next street. I knew parking would be difficult and standing in the sun for a long time to get in the building would be unpleasant, so I decided it wasn't worth it. I drove off and did whatever I decided to do with the rest of my day.

It wasn't right away that I regretted that decision, but over the years, when I think of what a cool experience that might have been, and would've had the bragging rights to say I was on the iconic and classic show Soul Train, even if only once. But those are the kinds of bad decisions you make when you're young because you lack foresight. To quote Mark Twain, "We regret the things we don't do more than the things we do."

JOB #7: LE CAFÉ ~ WAITRESS

During these early days, I was taking dance classes on a regular basis and managed to get a part-time, unpaid job working the front desk at a now-closed dance studio on 3rd Street in exchange for free dance classes. I was regularly going to auditions and trying to get an agent because I decided I should try to act in commercials too, even though I had no acting experience other than that one class I took in high school.

Getting an agent is a job in and of itself. Back then, long before the internet, many of us pursuing an agent would buy an agent's list from the Samuel French bookstore on Sunset (also no longer there) and do mass mailings of our black-and-white headshots with a resume full of lies stapled to the back of it. I never heard from anyone. Skip to twenty-five years later, and I landed my first agent, without even trying, through a friend.

This job took place in 1993, and I was hired as a waitress, but it didn't last long thanks to my inability to keep my mouth shut. The place was named Le Café, and it was on Ventura Boulevard in Encino, which is in the San Fernando Valley. This area of the Valley was new to me back then, and I've still never taken to it. It's kind of like the Beverly Hills of the Valley because there's a lot of money, big houses, and celebrities.

Le Café was a family-owned restaurant, and I have no idea how I found the job or how I got hired, but I remember the food was decent, and there was a jazz club upstairs that brought in a lot of big-name musicians. Sadly, I didn't work in the club, just the restaurant.

During the few weeks that I worked there, I waited on two celebrities. David Cassidy was really nice, and that made me happy, having watched *The Partridge Family* growing up. He was polite, smiled, looked at me when he ordered, and didn't act like a spoiled celebrity.

Unlike Mike Farrell, who played B.J. Hunnicut on M*A*S*H. He was the opposite: rude, demanding, unfriendly, entitled. As we all know, the way you treat a server says everything about who you are.

Here's what went down as the final blow to my employment. There was a dorky son who was one of the managers, and when he was talking to the servers at the pre-shift meeting about the house wines, I mentioned that one of the wines sucked, and he suddenly became furious. His face got all red, and he said, "You know what sucks? Your attitude! You're fired!" I was kind of shocked because he did it in front of everyone. I guess he felt that was fair since I said the wine sucked in front of everyone.

In retrospect, there may have been a few other incidents that led up to this, and he was perhaps right. My attitude sucked because I hated waiting tables, and it probably showed from time to time…or every shift. Also, in retrospect, I ask myself why I would say something like that, and I really don't have an answer other than I was a young idiot who, by the way, knew absolutely nothing about wine. That is all I remember about this job. After that unpleasant situation happened, I left, and it was back to pounding the pavement. I felt bad about getting fired again but had no idea there was so much more of that to come.

Looking back, I also think this is when my "programming" started to kick in, meaning all the messages I received growing up about money and my earning capability took hold. One of the messages I internalized was from my dad, who always used to say, "How are you going to get a good job without a college education?" Since I had no desire to go to college, I completely banked on becoming a rich and famous performer, but when you don't realize the power of programming or what messages you've been programmed with, you also don't realize that this is what can hold you back from realizing your potential.

Deep down, subconsciously, I didn't believe that I was capable of being more than a waitress, bartender, or receptionist because I grew up with the idea that a college education is how you got a "good" job and made "good" money. Of course, the conscious part of me knew that I was capable of making lots of money. Unfortunately, our subconscious mind, where our deepest beliefs are held, controls so much of what we do, and we don't even know it.

JOB #8: GRAPPA ~ BARTENDER

Grappa was a delicious, short-lived Italian restaurant on Sunset Boulevard at the corner of Sunset and Halloway, diagonal to where Tower Records used to be, and oh, how I miss Tower Records! It was a place where you could spend hours just perusing through an unbelievable collection of music. The Tower Records on the Sunset Strip was truly an iconic place because of the location as well as the many famous musicians that strolled through there.

It was also right across the street from the original Spago, where Wolfgang Puck made his name. I went to the original Spago once with two guys from the White Pelican and didn't understand the hype, but I don't understand a lot of things Hollywood hypes up. However, I met Wolfgang Puck at a New Year's Eve party in early 2000 that was held at the Beverly Hills Spago, and he and the food were both delightful!

Prior to being Grappa, it was the Old World restaurant, which had been there since the seventies. Since Grappa, it's been a couple of different places, including the Red Rock Bar and Isla Cantina, but they have settled on the State Social House since 2013.

When I got hired at Grappa, it was a brand-new restaurant with a cozy small bar area to the right of the entrance and the dining area to the left. It was elegantly decorated without being too stuffy and had a mix of booths and tables. The owners already had a very popular restaurant in Santa Monica named Vito, and I suppose they thought a location on Sunset Boulevard would be perfect. It should have been, but they had to compete with Marabelle, a very established and popular restaurant with a lot of Hollywood regulars that was literally next door. Sadly, Marabelle is gone now too.

Unfortunately, when I started, they already had a night bartender, so I got stuck with the day shift. I would occasionally get a decent lunch crowd at the bar, but it wasn't often enough that I made any real money, so I was always broke and still looking for or working at another job.

I worked the day shift with a waiter named Walid from Jordan. If you don't know anything about Jordan, that makes two of us. He was in California temporarily with a work visa but wanted to become a citizen and told me he would pay me $5,000 to marry him. Since I was making no money bartending, this was an idea I actually considered. It's funny looking back that I actually considered so little for my hand in marriage, but I was still far from realizing my value on many levels. I went so far as to talk to a lawyer about it. If I had been remotely attracted to him and if we were dating, I'm sure I would have gone through with it, but since I wasn't, it would have been a complete sham. Plus, the lawyer convinced me that we got caught, it would be a felony, and there could be fines and jail time. That's all I needed to hear. Jail is the only thing that keeps me from killing someone and the only reason I gave up shoplifting.

The other notable thing about Grappa was the manager that I would make out with after closing. A cute

Italian guy named Fernando who went on to open his own restaurant.

Yet again, business was not good at Grappa, and they started cutting shifts, so I had to find another job, and eventually, they closed. I don't even think the restaurant lasted more than three years, which is too bad because aside from the short time the Red Rock was there, they haven't had a good restaurant in that location since then, and it's prime real estate on Sunset.

Obviously, I was definitely taking lots of chances in the early nineties, but isn't that what youth is for—taking chances and making bad choices? I thought so.

Around the time I worked here, my friend Sarah and I went to a karaoke bar in Burbank called Dimples one night. I was always on the lookout for opportunities to perform, get on a stage, or hold a microphone because I *love* microphones. I think that's because in my family, everyone talks at once and interrupts each other. When I have a microphone, I have the power of volume.

Dimples had been around for years and was kind of a legendary place, and I'm sorry to say it was torn down a few years ago. We were drinking and singing songs, and after one of my songs, I got off the stage, and a guy approached me and told me I had a good voice. At this point, I had only sung in public one other time, which was in New Orleans when we were on our way across the country. But the reception to my performance from the crowd that night planted the seed for a singing career. When this guy told me I had a good voice, I was really happy because I had entertained pivoting from dancing to singing, even though I had no idea how to do that. What I did know was that my bad knees weren't going to keep me employed or unemployed as a dancer much longer.

    I told him I didn't have much experience and wanted to take voice lessons, and he recommended a voice teacher to me. He was a music engineer, or so he said. In L.A. people say they're all kinds of things they're not. I decided to call the voice teacher the next day and made an appointment with her. This officially launched my pursuit of a music career, which went on for ten years. I was twenty-six.

JOB #9: FELLINI'S ~ BARTENDER

Remember Goldschlager? That trendy, gross, cinnamon liqueur with gold flakes floating in it? I first tried it at Fellini's while working as a bartender there, and I'm sure that was the last place I drank it too. One day a friend mentioned something about a bar on Melrose Avenue, and suddenly this memory came flooding back, but it's not a vivid memory.

Fellini's originally opened in 1976, closed for a few years in the late eighties, became a club named Trinity for a while, and then reopened again as Fellini's in 1993. I worked there during Fellini's second life. It was named after the legendary Italian film director Federico Fellini, and it was a cool bar/restaurant with lots of dark wood and a long bar that drew a good crowd of regulars. This was another place where I got stuck with the lunch shift, which was usually hard for making decent money because sadly, at least in L.A., not a lot of people drink during lunch hour. Plus, it's usually over by three p.m., leaving you with about three hours to make your money. I'm sure that's why I didn't work there very long.

There was a small stage in the corner as soon as you came into the bar area, and some well-known people were said to have played there, like Bonnie Raitt, but it was probably most known for being used in the TV show *Melrose Place*. The exterior of Fellini's was used as the exterior for the bar "Shooters" on the show. That's probably not much of a fun fact if you weren't a fan of the show, but I was, and it was very popular at the time I worked there. It was also during the time that Melrose Avenue was still a very hip and fun place to hang out. Back then, it was full of trendy clothes and record stores, and it was a destination for shopping. I used to love to buy clothes on Melrose; it made me feel cool for some reason. It has since lost a lot of its former hipness and vibe, and now it's just a street I avoid driving down because of the traffic.

JOB #10: THE ROXBURY ~ WAITRESS

If you were in L.A. in the early nineties, *the* place to go was The Roxbury! It was one of the hottest restaurant/clubs in L.A. It was definitely a scene and the place to be seen, with a lot of celebrities, including Madonna and Tom Cruise, not to mention all the star fuckers who went there to party and try to mingle with celebrities. I'm not sure why, to be honest, because places like that are never really fun because they are always overpriced and overcrowded, but since celebrities went there, it automatically made it a draw. And it drew *a lot* of people.

The outside was brown and understated, and there was nothing special about the décor on the inside that I remember. There were two floors, a bar and dining room on both floors, but the dance floor was upstairs, so it was super loud upstairs. The type of L.A. crowd that the Roxbury drew was not my scene because they were entitled, demanding, unpleasant, and sometimes on drugs, so they could be really annoying. I didn't and I don't like helping people like that. And I've never liked the star fuckers because they act rude and just want to rub shoulders with celebrities, hoping some of their glitter will rub off on them. This was my first real glimpse into the celebrity crowd, and I didn't like it. I wasn't impressed with anyone just because they were famous. However, I knew a waitress could make a lot of money working there, so I applied, and they tried me out.

Things actually started okay. I did wait on Denzel

Washington while I was in training, who was nice enough from what I could tell. But I'll be honest; I was generally a good waitress, but I couldn't keep up with this place. This was when computers and point-of-sale systems were still fairly new to restaurants, and I hadn't worked on any yet. It was so hectic and fast-paced that I was "in the weeds," as they say in the restaurant business, for four days.

I had some guy training me who I could tell was getting really annoyed with me for being slow on the computer, and this wasn't the type of crowd you could afford to be slow with because they were overly expectant. So, after four days, I never heard back from them. I was never officially fired, but I got the message when they kept telling me I "wasn't on the schedule." Oh well!

With most places in L.A. having a short shelf life, The Roxbury closed in 1997 and reopened later as Miyagi's, a Japanese restaurant, which lasted a few years and then became the Pink Taco, which recently closed. Maybe you've heard of that *SNL* sketch and movie *A Night at the Roxbury* with Will Ferrell and Chris Katan? That is based on the legendary club where I spent four long nights lost in the glittery jungle with a tray in my hand.

JOB #11: SOME CLUB DOWNTOWN ~ TAXI DANCER

This next "job" I got through one of the cocktail waitresses I had worked with at the Crush Bar, that's if I can even consider this one a job.

It was somewhere in empty, sketchy downtown L.A., and I'm pretty sure it was a front for hookers who were getting some business here.

It sounded like a strange situation, but the girl who told me about it said there was good money to be made, and all I had to do was dance with some guys. Always needing money, I agreed. We dressed up and went downtown to this club where we parked in a sketchy-looking parking lot and walked up a long set of sketchy-looking stairs that led to a sketchy-looking room. Inside the room, there was a makeshift bar set up, although no alcohol was allowed. That was connected to a big dance floor with chairs surrounding it. The "bar" had fluorescent lighting above and served sodas and food like nachos, hotdogs, hamburgers, and individual bags of chips. There were a few chairs, tables, and small couches off to the side of the bar area for people to enjoy their weird food in this weird place. I was baffled by the whole setup and didn't even know clubs like this existed, so I was interested, confused, and suspicious all at the same time.

Slowly but surely, about twenty girls, of mixed levels of attractiveness and ethnicities, started filtering into the "dance room," where there was a DJ booth in the corner and red lighting all around. The girl I was with just instructed me to sit and wait.

"What are we waiting for?" I asked.

"Someone will ask you to dance," she casually replied.

Shortly after we sat down, men started arriving. Most of them were dressed in suits, and for some reason, I remember there were quite a few Asian men. One by one, they would approach one of the girls. The girl would stand up and follow the man to the dance floor, where they would start to slow dance. Some of the girls really played it up, laughing, flirting, and dancing sexy for the men. And some of the girls looked like they could be strippers, hookers, or both, so if they were, this would be an easy place to get customers and build their clientele. I remember watching and thinking how weird this was. After they danced for a while, the guy would "tip" them.

I was sitting there watching all of the girls get chosen to dance, and I know that I must have had some type of disgust or disapproval displayed on my face because I was uncomfortable with how strange the whole thing was. So much so that I was chosen last! I don't think I was the least attractive woman there, but I clearly was putting out a "don't ask me" vibe. I probably looked annoyed and was almost glad and insulted that I got picked last because I didn't want to do it and would have rather just observed the weirdness. But I ended up dancing with some guy for a few minutes, and he gave me twenty bucks.

I know one reason I didn't get asked to dance a lot was because I was silently judging the men who were willing to pay a stranger just to dance with them. I mean, how much of a loser do you have to be to pay someone who is fully dressed to dance with you? I went a few more times, but I never made the money the other girls were making, and more importantly, something felt dirty about it. Some of what I observed had such a sleazy, undertone that I knew I couldn't keep going. I also believed that I was capable of finding a job that wouldn't require me to dance with unfamiliar, desperate men.

Speaking of dancing gigs, while I was working there, I auditioned for the Janet Jackson world tour. I love Janet. I didn't make it to the final cut, and at the same time, I realized that even if I got the gig, I would never have been able to tour for a year or more doing such athletic dance routines. The choreography in the show, which I saw live, was physically intense. With my bad knees and my being prone to foot and joint injuries, I knew I had to change directions, and although I continued dancing for a while because I loved it, I was now focused primarily on singing opportunities while always on the prowl for a new job.

I was feeling pretty down about myself with the bad job situations and constantly being broke, and just to make matters worse, somewhere around this time, I made the mistake of missing a car payment. Being young and a little bit stupid, I didn't think missing one payment (two at most) would bring on the repo man.

After calling the police because I thought it was stolen, I found out that it had been repossessed and it was somewhere deep in the Valley. By the way, almost everyone in L.A. has a horror story involving getting their car towed, booted, impounded, or repossessed. The only way to get it back was to pay off the balance of roughly $3,000. Now, if I couldn't make a payment, I obviously didn't have $3,000 lying around, so I had to borrow it from a friend. When I found out where it was, I came face to face with the repo guy who stole my car, and then he proceeded to hit on me, which was infuriating! While at the repo place, he made a point of showing me his car that he seemed very proud of and pointed out the license plate, which I'll never forget: "IMKUWLK." It took me a minute to figure out that it was short for "I Make You Walk." So nice that this asshole took such pride in his car *and* his work.

It was a horrible experience, to say the least, but it was these types of experiences that made me become more responsible in the future. You can say I liked to learn things the hard way.

Looking back on these days, I can see how my thoughts and feelings about myself and my circumstances were dictating what was happening to me. The more dismal things got financially, the more I felt victimized, and the more that kept nailing in the bad messages I had about myself and money. So I kept creating even more of the same bad circumstances.

JOB #12: THE COMPANY I HAVE NO MEMORY OF ~ OFFICE CLERK

One day I was in an Uber and was having a pleasant chat with the driver about jobs we've had, and we happened to drive by a building I once worked in. I quickly blurted out, "I used to work in that building." It's one of the twin towers on the northwest side of Santa Monica and Sepulveda Boulevard.

Naturally, he asked the name of the company, and I couldn't remember. Then he asked me what kind of business the company was, and I couldn't remember that either. Then he asked what I did there, and guess what else I couldn't remember?

This job is such a faint memory that, for the most part, I only remember a couple of random things. Chances are, I wasn't there very long. In fact, I think it was only a temp job. I'm guessing it was some type of office assistant since it was in an office and there was already a receptionist, so I know I wasn't that.

I got the job from the roommate of a Cuban guy I was dating. His name was Ivan and I'm pretty sure he was a closeted gay man who was secretly in love with Ernesto, the Cuban. Ernesto was one of the hottest guys I've ever dated but dumb as a rock. At first, I thought it was just the language barrier since his English was compromised, but I eventually figured out that he was just hot and dumb. Too bad. He eventually went back to Miami, where he lived after coming from Cuba on a catamaran boat just a few years prior.

Here's what I remember: there was a pretty girl who did sales, there was another girl who talked about her vibrator like it was her boyfriend, and another girl who used to go to Lake Havasu a lot. Lake Havasu Girl was one of those bitchy girls who was mean to me at first but eventually came around once I made her laugh. I found out over time that laughter was the best way to disarm bitchy girls who hated me for no reason.

The thing I remember most about this job was that receptionist, Charlotte. She was so nice, and we got along famously. She was from Mississippi, and why I remember her so well is because once we had become friends, she told me the story of her daughter's father, who was a Black man. Charlotte was White, and apparently back in the eighties in parts of Mississippi, being White, in love, and getting pregnant by a Black man will get you disowned by your family. Charlotte hadn't talked to her family in ten years, and I couldn't believe it. It was the first time I met someone with a real story like that. To me, those were stories that you heard on *Oprah* or *Maury Povich*. They didn't happen to anyone I knew. I couldn't possibly imagine my family disowning me for loving someone, regardless of their color or sex, religion, etc. I don't remember all the horrible details of her story but I remember Charlotte, her bright personality, and her beautiful daughter, who I met once when she was about ten. Her story really had an impact on me, and I admired her strength for choosing to move on with her life because she knew her family's attitude and behavior was wrong. She moved to L.A. and never looked back. I didn't work at this job long, maybe a few months, but Charlotte left an impression on me. So did the Cuban, but I never saw either one of them again.

As far as my performing life, now that I was taking voice lessons, I was always looking for opportunities to practice singing live with a piano player at a legitimate open mic. Of course, in L.A., there are lots of opportunities for performers. I regularly attended the open mic at The Dresden, a legendary place, not just because it was in the movie *Swingers* but also because of the dynamic duo of Marty and Elayne, who played there for close to forty years. They were a husband-and-wife team that everyone loved and were true L.A. legends. Sadly, Marty died in 2021.

The open mic was on Tuesday nights, and because Marty and Elayne knew almost all of the standards, you just needed to tell them your key, and they would accompany you. Marty on the drums and Elayne on the keyboard and flute—what a great time! The Dresden is such an amazing place because there is the bar side and the restaurant side, and the restaurant side has large booths and décor that makes you feel like you're back in time in 1940s Hollywood. Meanwhile, the bar area has a Sixties vibe with the paneling on the walls, small cocktail tables, and martinis in everyone's hands. The bartenders are the kind of guys who have been slinging drinks for forty years, specializing in dirty martinis, and can easily whip up outdated drinks like Pink Squirrels and Brandy Alexanders.

It was a great place to do an open mic because there

was always a crowd, especially after *Swingers*, and it was good experience for me trying to keep up with Marty and Elayne, who tended to play their own unique versions of songs. Before The Dresden was featured in the movie, it was less crowded and more fun because it was like a hidden gem that not everyone knew about. I found out about it a few years before the movie came out by an ex-boyfriend, so I got to enjoy it before *Swingers* made it a popular destination for everyone, including tourists.

There was another open mic I would go to on Lankershim Boulevard in North Hollywood, and back then, it was a quaint little gay bar/restaurant that had an open mic with a piano player after dinner hour. I would show up with my sheet music and do my little song, and one night, Rich, the bartender, asked me if I wanted to be in a band he was putting together. He said he played guitar and knew a drummer and bass player and was looking for female singers. Naturally, I jumped at the chance! A band? This was exciting! The type of music? Blues and soul! I was thrilled!

He eventually brought in another singer and a strange keyboard player, and I brought in my friend Marilyn, who I knew from Universal. Now we had a full band with three female singers. I had the idea of putting together a Tina Turner-style background dance routine since the movie *What's Love Got to Do With It?* had come out. All of us could dance, and I love Tina Turner, so it only made sense to try and emulate her as I sang "Proud Mary" as one of my solos. Tina will always be one of my performing idols. I saw her twice in concert, and she was fabulous! To me, the true test of a great performer is what they do live. Anyone can sound good in a recording studio, but not anyone can be a great live performer, but Tina was…*simply the best!*

We rehearsed at this scary rehearsal studio downtown where lots of other bands rehearsed. It was my first experience in a rehearsal studio like that, and I loved it. We would walk down the dimly lit, rundown hallways, hearing drummers pounding, guitars screeching, singers wailing, and all kinds of other sounds before we got into our room to practice making our own noise. It was a fun time! We called ourselves "Midnight Rhythm." It's kind of a stupid band name, but there are lots of those, so we were just another mediocre band with a bad name.

The first gig we ever did was at Moonshadows in North Hollywood. I invited everyone I knew, including all of my dancer friends from Universal. Between all of us in the band, we packed the place with our friends and anyone else who was there unknowingly. And even though we weren't that great a band, we rocked the place! We thought we were amazing, and everyone's excitement matched our enthusiasm. There really is nothing like live performance. I think that is one reason why I never pursued acting in film and TV as much as I did live performance. It's my need for instant gratification.

That was the first of a few bands that I was in over the next several years, and it was a great first experience.

JOB #13: B.B. KING'S BLUES CLUB ~ WAITRESS

The dance job at Universal was seasonal, so some of these jobs took place while I was still working at Universal part-time, including this one. I got word that a new club was opening at Universal CityWalk, which is essentially an overly ambitious outdoor mall connected to the theme park. It's hard to believe CityWalk didn't even exist when I first started working at Universal. It was built in 1993, so it was still pretty new when this job came along, and nothing like it is now. Those of us who worked at the theme park were happy once it was built because we were within walking distance of a few new bars and restaurants that were just steps from the entrance of the theme park.

Back then there were only a few restaurants, including Tony Roma's and a Mexican restaurant named Camacho's, the movie theaters, and a few little stores. A lot of us went to Camacho's because it was more of a fun place to hang out than Tony Roma's, but every year they expanded it, and there would be more stores and restaurants. Eventually, they added a Hard Rock Café on the far end of CityWalk, which was a big attraction for years until it closed in 2020. Live music started to become a regular thing that would happen outside of the Hard Rock. Through the years, they added other popular chain restaurants that varied in flavor and style, like Jimmy Buffet's Margaritaville and a Buca di Beppo, to name a few, and now there are more than thirty restaurants! There are also typical mall-type stores like Abercrombie & Fitch, Sephora, Billabong, and of course, a Universal Studios store so you can buy overpriced items just because they say "Universal Studios" on them. Overall, today CityWalk is a collection of pricey stores, mediocre restaurants, loud noises, visual stimulation, and various forms of entertainment.

In 1995, the newly built B.B. King's, which was on the second floor of CityWalk, was having "open call" interviews, which meant anyone looking for a waiter or bartending job in L.A. showed up to apply. At the time, I was doing the mouse show in the theme park and had been doing it for four years, but it was at the end of summer, and the show would be closing, not just for the season but permanently, so I didn't want to miss the opportunity to get a regular gig. I remember changing out of my mouse costume and into appropriate interview clothes while still sweaty and running back and forth in between shows to try and get an interview. It took me three trips back and forth. The manager who hired me told me later he appreciated my hustle, and that's why I got the job. Unfortunately, I didn't get hired as a bartender. I was hired as a waitress, and that was a much harder job, especially in this particular club/restaurant.

They hired a large crew of young wannabes like me made up of actors, singers, dancers, writers, etc.—the typical Hollywood restaurant front-of-house staff mixed in with some young management guys, most in their early thirties.

What could go wrong?

It was a very cool place that was decorated in what I would describe as a New Orleans kind of bluesy style.

There were three floors, a full bar on every floor, and large photos hung on the walls of famous blues and soul legends like B.B. King (of course), Otis Redding, and Willie Dixon, among others. The tables were set up against the railings on the second and third floors so that you could see the amazing stage. The stage was about four feet above the first-floor tables, so everyone had a good view of the stage, whether you were looking up from the first-floor tables or looking down from the second or third floor, and it had an amazing sound system for live music. They served typical Southern dishes like fried chicken, collard greens, and cornbread. I gained a few pounds while working there because I couldn't keep my hands off of the cornbread with honey butter. Running up and down three floors every night wasn't enough to compensate for all the cornbread I was eating during my shifts.

Once it opened, it was complete chaos. Initially, it did really well and was often packed, but management had not figured out a smooth system for anything, so things went wrong all the time. The food runners would deliver food to the wrong table on the wrong floor, or the kitchen would run out of simple items like sour cream—it's very awkward to tell someone who just ordered a baked potato that there was no sour cream. Orders would get put into the computer wrong, and the chefs would go crazy. Waiters got into fights over the smallest things because everyone was stressed out all the time, and the fact that there were three floors made it worse because everything took extra effort. For example, if you were working on the third floor and forgot someone's side of ranch dressing, there was a lot of exercise involved to fix that. Waiters were bumping into each other constantly running up and down the stairs until finally, management put a small kitchen area on the third floor so we could at least keep some backup items like condiments, which saved a lot of time.

Despite the chaos, we were making good money. Some of us would work a Saturday night and turn around and come in the next morning for Sunday Gospel Brunch, and although we were usually tired and slightly hungover, we would walk away with about $500 for two days, which was good for a server back in 1995.

One of the best things about working there was seeing some of the blues bands that performed. I was lucky enough to see B.B. King himself perform, as well as some other greats like Percy Sledge, Mavis Staples, and John Lee Hooker. It was a big club but still had an intimate feel to it even with a stage big enough to comfortably fit B.B. King's whole band, which included a second guitarist, a drummer, a keyboard player, a bass player, and a three-piece horn section.

A really cool thing they did at this club was to hold a talent show at the employee Christmas party. Because so many of the staff were also performers, they let us put on a show doing whatever our particular talent was. For example, a writer put together a short play, and a few of the waiters who were also actors performed it. Lots of musicians played, and since I was in my first band at the time, I asked management if I could bring them in to play with me, and they said yes. I got to perform on B.B. King's stage, and we played "Proud Mary" Tina Turner style.

It was a very cool venue to perform in. Every time I was waiting tables and a band was on the stage performing, I felt a little envious. After the Christmas party, a few people said to me, "Why are you waiting tables?" suggesting that I should be making money as a singer. I wish it were that easy, but as someone who was segueing from a career in dance to a music career, this was a great place to work. I got to hear live blues every night and see a huge variety of performers and musicians. I also met a person who forever influenced my life.

He was a drummer in the house band at the time, and I learned later that he played with a who's who of artists, including Stevie Wonder, Chaka Khan, Bryan Ferry, Slash, Robin Trower, and Dave Mason, among many others. The first time I heard him play, I waited for him to get off the stage and walked up to him and told him how much I loved his playing. This started a conversation that turned into a friendship that eventually turned into a relationship that lasted for eight years. I'm hesitant to name him for my own reasons, but he taught me more about music than I could have learned in any class. He helped me write songs and eventually produced a record I made. He is, in part, the reason I know what I know about music because we would sit and talk about it for hours, and he would explain things to me so that I could be a better singer and songwriter. I got to meet, listen to, and even play with some incredible musicians because of him. He will always be a very important influence on my life as a whole.

Back to the restaurant. One of the problems with the poor management led to a revolving door of employees, including various managers. It started off with a great core group of staff, but because of the disorganization, people started leaving or getting fired, and it never seemed to get into a solid place. I worked there for almost two years, but business started to drop off and there were rumors that they were having financial problems, and like so many other restaurants in L.A., they had a shelf life, and it wasn't that long. The money we started making during shifts went way down, and most of the people that were there since the opening—and there weren't many of us left—started looking for other jobs.

Still, it was a fun place while it lasted, with a lot of shenanigans between the employees. I remember making out with one of the other waiters in the walk-in cooler, and two staff members allegedly had sex in the third-floor manager's office, which was the size of a phone booth. Several of us would go next door to Lucille's (which was named after B.B. King's guitar) after our shift and get drunk together. I am still in touch with one of my friends from there who I love dearly but is now living on the other side of the world.

Meanwhile, after about ten gigs together, my first band broke up, and it was mostly because the drummer got a gig with Yngwie Malmsteen, the Swedish speed metal guitar player. We also couldn't find a good, permanent keyboard player, and one of the singers was unreliable, so it just eventually fell apart.

I soon got a chance to join a new band which was formed out of a musical event for a benefit that was held at B.B. Kings. One of the promoters of the event knew me from the club and asked me to sing in it. It was an all-day event, and many female singers and musicians performed throughout the day to raise money for a cause. After meeting each other and appreciating the combined talent of all the women involved, a few people organized a meeting for any of the female performers who were interested in forming a band. The result was a fourteen-piece all-female blues band that included a horn section and several singers.

After multiple rehearsals and the first gig, which was at a tiny club in North Hollywood called The Blue Saloon, a lot of drama started almost immediately. It sadly turned into a situation where one of the singers, who thought she was the strongest vocally, and she probably was, felt threatened by a couple of the other singers. Me being one of them. That competitive drama divided all of us and the band eventually split into two groups, one called Women in Blues (which I was in), and I can't remember what the others called themselves.

Women in Blues played in some of L.A.'s best clubs, like The House of Blues, The Troubadour, and The Baked Potato. These were some of my favorite performances because of the venues. The House of Blues was such a cool club; everything from the look of the stage to the details of the interior decoration felt like rock and roll, and when I was in the green room before the shows and performing on that stage, I truly felt like I was living my dream.

The Troubadour is another legendary place I feel lucky to have played in. Although there's nothing fancy about it, it still has a cool vibe with a stage that is raised about four feet with standing room only on the first floor, but it also has a small balcony that overlooks the stage. It's the same club where Elton John, at twenty-three, rocked the stage one night back in 1970, and his career changed overnight. The Troubadour is still standing and still hosting bands looking for their big break. The Baked Potato is a tiny little club, about the size of someone's living room, but with great sound, enough that it draws well-known musicians, especially jazz musicians.

Although being in Women in Blues was another relatively short-lived situation, I had a wonderful time playing with those women, and I learned a lot about musicians, singers, and egos.

After B.B. King's closed down, I think it was another business for a while, but it later became the Jon Lovitz Comedy Club, and I performed there as a comedian several years later. It was just as good a club for comedy as it was for music because of the setup and sound system, and I loved doing stand-up there too. It's kind of cool that I performed on that stage in two different capacities and had a great time every time.

JOB #14: LUNARIA ~ CATER WAITER

Since I mentioned Stevie Wonder in a previous story, let me brag for a second about when I met him. First, some backstory. When I was ten years old, I watched Stevie Wonder win the Grammy for Record of the Year for *Songs in the Key of Life*. I loved a couple of songs on the album, so I begged my dad for the money to buy it. I had to beg because it was a whopping $15 for a double album, but I was a good beggar, so he gave me the money. It was the first album I ever bought and still one of my favorite records of all time.

Cut to the nineties. My sister and I are working as cater waiters at a jazz club named Lunaria in Century City. We were setting up for a holiday party, and a guy walked in who I recognized from B.B. King's. His name was Curtis, and he had worked as a cook when I was a waitress. Now he was working for KJLH, the radio station owned by Stevie Wonder. After we said our hellos, he told me that Stevie would be coming to the party.

I couldn't believe it; I was so excited I could barely contain myself. After everything was set up and people were seated, in walks Stevie Wonder in a bright aqua suit, and I was just mesmerized. Here was my childhood music icon right here in the same room as me (and I didn't have to chase him down the street)! I made it a point to get close to him as often as I could by clearing dishes at his table or refilling the water.

At one point, the man sitting next to him told me he liked my perfume and asked me if I could lean in so that

Stevie could take a whiff. *Oh my God! I am being asked to let Stevie Wonder smell me!* Naturally, I leaned in as close as I could without sitting on his lap or kissing him, and after breathing me in, Stevie Wonder told me how nice I smelled. That's when I took the opportunity to tell him what he meant to me. He got a big smile on his face and thanked me. It was a moment I'll never forget.

So even though being a cater waiter sucked because the work was sporadic and the money wasn't great, it provided me with a magical moment that I cherish. And I don't know the catering company I got the job with, and I don't know if I ever did a gig with them again, but I believe the universe works like that. It brought me to Stevie, whose music I will always love and who liked the way I smelled.

Had I known anything about manifesting back in those days, I would have recognized that meeting Stevie Wonder was a manifestation of something I dreamed about since I was ten years old. Same with Gene Kelly. As a dancer, he was one of my idols, and here I was, roughly five years or so in Los Angeles, and I had met two of my biggest idols. So many fun experiences were happening when it came to entertainment, but so many hard experiences were still happening when it came to day jobs and money.

One of those fun experiences happened right around the same time, when I worked as an extra on Snoop Dogg's "Murder Was the Case" video. The video was shot at an old, abandoned prison east of downtown L.A., and it was a night shoot. All of the extras were just sitting around because you do a lot of that on set when the production manager came over to us and told us he wanted us to make "picket" signs as if we were protesting Snoop being in jail as part of the video. They provided us with poster board, markers, etc. and we got to work. A little while later he came back to check on our signs, and he liked mine so much that he showed it to Snoop, who laughed. I simply wrote "Doggy Style."

JOB #15: THE CENTURY CLUB ~ WAITRESS

The Century Club, at the time I worked there in the mid-nineties, was one of the biggest clubs in the city. I got this job because I knew one of the managers who I worked with at B.B. King's; he had been working at the Century Club for a while. At the time, it was owned by Mark Fleischman, who also owned Studio 54 *after* its heyday. It was a sprawling space with two floors that contained a large dance floor and a stage in the main room. There were several bars throughout the property and also a large outdoor area with seating where they would set up stations for cooking burgers and hotdogs after hours. It was a fine dining restaurant between five and nine but turned into a club after dinner hours. It had a variety of acts and performers, including Bruce Willis and his band, Teena Marie, and Kid Creole and the Coconuts, among others. Although it was a nice enough club, it wasn't a club that booked A-list talent, and the crowd that was attracted to The Century Club was the L.A. club crowd. Not my favorite crowd.

You may have noticed by now, I generally don't like *any* crowds.

This was a place I told a customer off for bad tipping and then immediately ratted myself out to the manager before the customer could rat on me. I knew I had given the table good service, and they gave me a two percent tip. I couldn't hold back.

I walked up to the table and asked, "Was there a problem with the service because you only left me two percent?"

The jerk proceeded to tell me that I didn't check on them enough, which I knew was bullshit, and I responded by telling him that if he "couldn't afford to tip properly on good service, then he shouldn't be going out to dinner."

I stand by that statement. To all the people who dine out, if you can't afford to tip well, then stay home! I think it should be a law that everyone must wait tables for at least one month of their life, and then maybe people would know how to act at a restaurant. I've even had friends who have never waited tables say, "They're just bringing you food." And I would have to correct them. No, they are not just bringing you food; they are "waiting" on you, which means bringing you food and drinks, clearing your table, cleaning up after you, and providing a service that you don't get when you stay at home. So pay for it!

I immediately found the manager and told her what happened, and she said, "If you do that again, you're fired," but she also thought it was kind of funny because she knew I was a good waitress.

I didn't work there that long, and I ended up quitting because I wasn't getting enough shifts. I don't have tons of memories from here other than briefly waiting on Wilt Chamberlain. I really wanted to ask him how he kept count of the twenty thousand women he claimed to have slept with. Did he have a little black book the size of a phone book or some filing cabinets? I mean, how do you keep track of that many people? But I wasn't ballsy enough to ask a seven-foot former NBA star his method for managing so many sexcapades. I also waited on Kool and the Gang, but I don't think the whole gang was there. Just Kool.

This was one of several waiting jobs that I had to leave because of a shortage of shifts and lack of money. It was a constant theme in my life: always job hopping to make more money because I couldn't live on one job but not finding two jobs that worked out schedule-wise while pursuing my performing gigs or auditions and the like.

Such is the life of an artist in L.A.

JOB #16: GLADSTONES ~ WAITRESS

This was a waiting job that I took at one of the many times I was desperate. Sadly, so many people in L.A. experience desperation—just ask any performer or aspiring writer. L.A. is filled with the stereotypical "struggling artist," and I felt like I was a poster girl for that stereotype.

I worked at Gladstones after the Century Club, and interestingly enough, it was located on Universal CityWalk, not far from B.B. King's.

When it came to working at Gladstones, there were several things I didn't like about it, not to mention I was really sick of waiting tables, so of course, my attitude was less than positive. Also, it was a seafood restaurant, and I hate fish, which left my food picking to a minimum. It was also a sprawling restaurant that offered huge servings of gross, fried seafood that we carried on giant trays that were heavy from the weight of the plates, the metal lids that kept the food hot, and of course, all that breading on the fried food. So, it was a more physically demanding serving job than I had before, including when I had to run up and down the stairs at B.B. King's.

In the entranceway, they had a huge barrel full of peanuts that customers could eat as they waited for their tables, and they were allowed to just drop the shells on the floor, if that tells you anything. There was usually a long wait for a table, and it's a perfect example of how tourists are always drawn to the worst places because they just don't know any better.

As a new hire, I always got stuck in the section that

was furthest from the kitchen, so I ran my ass off all night. I did lose some weight while working there, but that was the only good thing about it.

The uniform was hideous! White jeans, a blue-and-white-striped shirt, and red *suspenders!* It was such a stupid outfit, and I was always paranoid that people I knew would see me, so naturally that happened regularly. I think the entire time I worked there I was stuck in the section that was outside on the patio area where all the tourists and Universal employees who had known me as a dancing mouse could see me sweating as I delivered giant plates of fried shrimp and tartar sauce. It was humiliating.

I have no good memories of this job. I didn't make any new friends there, the food was subpar, the money wasn't great, and I walked around in that stupid uniform all night. I worked here for about six months and was miserable the whole time, so I was on the lookout for a new opportunity and thought I came across a good one. But I was wrong.

What I didn't realize at the time was how my miserable attitude kept me living the same cycle of working jobs I didn't want, then focusing on how much I didn't want it, always struggling for money, and then focusing on my lack of it.

And I kept repeating this cycle.

JOB #17: MOONLIGHT TANGO CAFÉ ~ WAITRESS

I really wanted to stop waiting tables altogether, but when I saw an ad that wanted "waiters who could sing," I was interested. The Moonlight Tango Café was a restaurant on Ventura Boulevard in the San Fernando Valley that put on a show similar to a dinner theater. Traditional dinner theater usually includes a meal while you watch a play or musical. This was a place where people would have dinner while watching a variety of singing waiters get on stage and perform different songs along with a small band...in between taking orders and delivering food! I thought it was right up my alley.

Something about the restaurant was reminiscent of older days, and it was kind of funky and cheesy at the same time. The woman who managed it—who looked like she had spent years in dinner theater—told me I should wear more makeup because they wanted everyone who worked there to look theatrical. I didn't like wearing a lot of makeup, but I begrudgingly did my hair and slapped on some extra makeup, hoping that would help. That still didn't get me enough shifts. I really wanted to work there because I was always looking for opportunities to perform, so I thought this would be a good way to make money *and* get stage time. Even though the clientele was mostly older people, and the setting wasn't ideal with dishes, glasses, and silverware clanking constantly, all stage time was valuable!

The schedule was always posted very last minute, and

we had to call in to see if we were on. There was no stability or guaranteed shifts whatsoever. I was barely making any money because I was only given the slow nights and an occasional weekend because the weekends were reserved for the waiters who had been there longer. I was essentially a backup, and that wasn't making me much money. Then the shifts started dwindling even more, and I was down to two shifts in the middle of the week. It seemed like no matter what restaurant I was working in, I kept getting these leftover shifts, and I was really getting tired of it.

After not giving me any decent shifts since I was hired and still waiting for an opportunity to sing, Christmas Eve rolled around, and they called me into work at the last minute. I was really annoyed because I love Christmas Eve more than Christmas Day. It always felt more Christmasy to me, and I wanted to hang out with my brother and sister. I felt a sense of obligation because it was my job, so I got dressed in my uniform and got in my car.

As I was driving, I got angrier and angrier thinking that because they couldn't find anyone else to come in and thought that I was so desperate for shifts, they could just *use* me whenever they wanted. So, I drove to the restaurant, walked in, and quit! In retrospect, I should have told them I wasn't available and took my chances of getting fired, but I was much more impulsive in those days and didn't always handle things in the most mature way.

When I left the restaurant and got in my car, I had one of those scared but relieved feelings. After all, I wasn't making much money or getting to sing much there, but now here I was out of work once again. I went back home and had a nice Christmas with my brother, my sister, and my bottle of vodka, and almost forgot about that job altogether.

Have you noticed a pattern yet? I was constantly in and out of jobs that were never stable and/or never enough money. I also had such self-limiting beliefs as to what I was really capable of when it came to a job. My mentality was, "This isn't what I really want to do, so who cares?" My attitude was so backwards because I didn't treat any of the jobs that made me money as important because I just wanted to be a performer. But I wasn't making money doing that, and instead of treating my job with respect, I treated it like I didn't care about it. That attitude kept me broke and just attracted more bad circumstances. Horrible bosses included.

JOB #18: SYLVIA'S ~ CATERING AND ASSISTANT

My sister Kris found a job working as an assistant and catering manager for a woman named "Sylvia" who owned a restaurant named "Sylvia's" on 3rd Street. It was a cute restaurant with roughly twenty tables, but she did a huge catering business as well. I will say that Sylvia's food was spectacular. Some of the stand-out dishes she was known for were her fried chicken and the blackberry cobbler, which were always requested on catering jobs. Kris seemed to like working for her and was learning things from Sylvia that would eventually help her in opening her own restaurant in Maine in 2001.

However, Kris told me some stories about Sylvia and her temper and how she would yell at the chef, at the waiters, at the vendors, and everyone else...though she never seemed to treat Kris that way. I worked a couple of catering jobs with Kris, so I became familiar with how things worked. After a few months, Kris decided to return to Maine and suggested that I take over her position at the restaurant. I had met Sylvia, so she was familiar with me and decided to give me the position since she had been happy with Kris.

Since I had been out of work again, I happily took the job when Kris went back east, and at first, everything was fine.

Until I started to see the temper that Kris had told me about.

Sylvia was an unstable and angry person who would insult and berate people and was straight-up abusive to her employees. The waiters were usually aspiring models and actors who were always good-looking men. She never hired women servers. In fact, I think Kris and I were the only women who worked there, and that eventually turned into a problem. Kris and I have very different personalities and physical appearances, as Kris is very passive and nonthreatening to women. Let's just say that I'm the opposite of that to some women. I was thirty years old and in pretty good shape from dancing. Sylvia was roughly forty-five years old and had been very overweight for a while. The waiters flirted with me, the chef and I got along very well, and I believe Sylvia's perception of these situations possibly fueled some crazy behavior. Like weird, jealous behavior.

The job consisted of everything from managing the catering jobs to running errands like picking up flowers for the restaurant and paying the vendor bills. It was a decent amount of responsibility, but I was doing a good job from what I could tell, and she didn't seem to have any complaints with my job performance. I was working for her during the summer months, and being that it was so hot, I asked her if I could wear shorts to work. She told me that I could as long as I stayed in the back office and didn't go out into the restaurant because it didn't look professional.

A few days later I came to work wearing shorts that I bought at the GAP. A couple of hours after I got there, Sylvia came walking into the office, and I could tell she was in a bad mood. The first thing she said was, "What are you wearing?"

I said, "What do you mean?"

"You look like a whore," she said.

"Excuse me! You said I could wear shorts when it was hot out."

"Go home and get changed," she said. "You're not getting paid for today, and don't ever come in here again looking like a whore."

I looked at her for a second in shock, and then I got up, dropped the keys to the office on the desk, and walked out. I think she was equally shocked by my unwillingness to tolerate her abuse because she didn't say anything.

This is one of the few times I quit a job for obvious reasons because there is no amount of money I will accept so that someone can abuse me. People go to work every day and tolerate abuse and bad behavior from their bosses, and it's bullshit. No job is worth your self-esteem, and no amount of money is worth your dignity. How dare she tell me that I wouldn't get paid because of my clothes?

The problem was now I couldn't get unemployment because I had quit, and when I applied and explained the situation, they still denied me. This was an important lesson: if you're in a bad job, always try to get fired instead of quitting because you can't get unemployment if you quit. In this case, I didn't have a choice.

However, I couldn't just let that go. I wanted to exact revenge because I was so angry since I was out of a job and couldn't get unemployment.

Also, by the way, since when do whores shop at the GAP?

What I really wanted to do was throw a brick through

the windshield of her BMW, but I didn't want to commit a crime. Well, it turns out that someone waited until the weekend when it was busy, drove down close to the restaurant, and parked on a side street. This unknown person crept down the alley behind the restaurant where she parked her car and was dressed in all black, ninja style, so no one would see them, and then took a few really long nails and stuck them in her tires. They never found out who it was.

Cut to 2015, twenty years or so after I walked out. I was walking around West Hollywood, and guess who I saw? She was walking her mangy, little dog, and I don't think she noticed me, but I could never forget her ugly, mean face. I found out several years later that she was sued twice for sexual harassment by a couple of servers who worked for her. I don't know if she went out of business or closed it down, but the restaurant is long gone, and the memories live on.

JOB #19: SAND DOLLAR GRILL ~ L.A. INTERLUDE

After losing another job in L.A., my sister Kris suggested I come to Maine for the summer and work to give myself a break from the grind of job hunting yet again. Kris was living in Bar Harbor, which is a seasonal town, and come summer, there are usually a lot of restaurant jobs to be had for a few months. I got there in June and within a few days got hired as a waitress in one of the town's few fine dining restaurants, The Sand Dollar Grill.

It was a charming restaurant that had been a large, private home at one time, and there was seating on the first and second floors. Since it had been a residence, it had a very cozy vibe with a lot of wood and beautiful crown moldings. The floors were original hardwood but pristinely refinished and always shining. The small but tasteful wooden bar was against the back wall of the restaurant, and the kitchen was behind that. It was tastefully decorated and had excellent food.

The owner was an uptight guy named Tom who I am convinced was a closet homosexual. He had been married to a woman, and I always thought the woman's sexuality was also questionable. He was extremely particular about everything from how you handled the glassware when placing it on the table to how you opened a wine bottle. The other servers had been working there for previous seasons, so they knew how he was, but I was new to this kind of super uptight environment, and I struggled with it. I had worked in fine dining in L.A., so I was completely familiar with dealing with entitled, picky people but never dealt with a restaurant owner who was so uptight about weird details that had nothing to do with service but more with an image he was trying to project. I understand the importance of image, but he was always on the verge of his head exploding.

One night we were really busy, and a lot of my tables were ordering wine, so he decided to jump in and help by bringing one of my tables their wine selection. I appreciated the help because opening wine in a fine dining restaurant is always a ceremony, so it takes time, but I made a big mistake. I accidentally sent him to the wrong table, and when he presented the wine to the customers and they informed him that it wasn't the wine they chose, he walked away from the table. As I saw him approaching me, I could see his face was turning so purple that I thought blood was going to squirt out of his eyes. It was a simple mistake that any normal person would have brushed off, but he was so embarrassed by this accident that he brought me back into the kitchen and yelled at me in front of everyone. All because he went to the wrong table.

Strike one!

After that happened, my attitude changed, and I would show up for work caring less than I had before about him, his restaurant, or his stupid, uptight bullshit. A week or two later, one of the other waiters and I were behind the bar polishing glassware and talking about martinis and Manhattans. Tom was in the dining area listening in and said something about sweet vermouth in a martini (or something like that). Considering I had been to bartending school and now hated him, I couldn't stop myself from correcting him. He disagreed with me, and I insisted that he was wrong.

Strike two!

I had to back down because he was getting so pissed, but I've never had a problem confronting people in authority positions, especially if they publicly humiliated me. Now I was on shaky ground, though. I knew it but it was getting closer to the end of the season, so I knew he kind of still needed me because it wouldn't be easy to find a new waiter this late in the season, and I kind of still needed the job to save money before going back to LA. But then, one day I called in sick because I wasn't feeling well.

Strike three!

He fired me. I didn't really care because things had gotten so uncomfortable there that it wasn't even worth the money. A couple of weeks later, I packed up my clothes and went back to L.A.

The one good thing that came out of this job was my friend Monica, who was also a waitress there. I wasn't sure if I liked her at first because she seemed a little uptight, but I soon realized she acted that way around Tom because everyone did and that she actually was really funny. We had some good times drinking together that summer and are still friends to this day. It was a fun summer, but I was ready to go back to L.A., even though I dreaded job hunting again.

At least while I was in Maine working at this job I didn't like, I kept working on music. I found a guitar player who learned a couple of cover songs I liked singing, and we put on a couple of performances at one of the bar/restaurants in town called The Lompoc, and that was really fun. I always needed something artistic to balance out my dislike for the jobs I had to do to pay my bills.

JOB #20: T MINUS 30 ~ PRODUCTION ASSISTANT

Luckily, once I was back in L.A., I didn't have to hunt for long because I got this job from a referral. T Minus 30 was a commercial production company in Venice on Abbot Kinney, which is now a total hot spot. Back then, it was popular but still had a hippie/surfer vibe that made it a great place to be. Now it has a little of that mixed in with a hipster/influencer vibe.

If you don't know what a PA (production assistant) does, they are the gopher for the office or the production or whatever the situation is. They are the lowest person on the production totem pole and get bossed around by just about everyone. The rank on a production is the producer at the top, then the production manager, followed by the production coordinator. Below all of them is the PA.

I was the office PA.

That meant my job was answering the phone at times, running errands, stocking the kitchen area, making the coffee, emptying trash, and basically doing anything else that the producers, production managers, or coordinators would never do because that would be "below them." This was also my first production job and I quickly learned that behind the scenes is not for me. I found it to be boring, and all the people who worked in production just seemed to be doing what looked like regular office jobs. It didn't seem creative, so I wasn't really interested in it, but I have major respect for production people because they make so much happen…even if most of them seem uptight.

I remember quite a few people from this job, considering how long ago it was. The owner was a decent, understated guy, and there were a couple of female producers on staff who were okay but leaned toward bitchy. There was a production manager who used to start all of her statements with "FYI," a production coordinator who smelled like pee and cigarettes, and another coordinator who I liked a lot and didn't smell bad.

But the main person from this job who had a big impact on my life was the receptionist, Shelly. Not only are we still friends to this day, but she made me a better person just by being her. Shelly was diagnosed with muscular dystrophy at a young age and has been in a wheelchair for a long time. For as long as I've known her, she has just been a sweet, positive, and loving human being. Whenever I think I am going through something difficult, I think about Shelly, because she made me realize that no matter what you're going through, you can always keep a positive attitude. I will always be grateful for this job because of meeting Shelly.

I think I worked there for less than a year when, once again, business slowed down and they had to lay people off.

Back on unemployment!

When I tell you that I was broke a lot, I don't mean I had five bucks in my bank account; I mean that one time I paid for a half dozen eggs with nickels. Do you know what kind of a strange and confused look you get from the checkout person when you're paying with nickels? It's one step up from pennies. I obviously had already spent the quarters and dimes.

While my brother and I were still living together and had no money, our only affordable form of entertainment was renting a movie, getting a six-pack of beer, a bag of Doritos, and a joint. In retrospect, all I can say is that when you're able to have fun with no money, you're still rich in a way. Of course, I didn't realize that back then because I was only focused on my lack of money, which was part of the problem.

JOB #21: DIMILLO'S FLOATING RESTAURANT ~ BARTENDER ~ L.A. INTERLUDE

After another year of struggle in L.A. and getting fired from my latest job, my sister Kris, who was now living in Portland, Maine, suggested I come and live with her again for the summer. I loved Portland, so this sounded like a fun idea to me.

One day while walking along the waterfront, I noticed DiMillo's Floating Restaurant (now called DiMillo's on the Water). I didn't know at the time the interesting history of this former boat, now restaurant. Originally named "The New York" in 1941, it ran as a car ferry between New Castle, Delaware, and Pennsville, New Jersey. Over the years it was bought and sold several times until the DiMillo family bought it in 1980 and turned it into a restaurant in 1982. It is over two hundred feet long and can seat up to six hundred guests, including the outside decks.

When I walked in, I immediately liked it because I love boats and restaurants, so the combination is even better. I walked into the bar area and saw the very long, beautiful, wooden bar that had stools lining both sides and windows that ran along the entire bar area so you could see the other boats and the harbor. It felt cozy and nautical, two of my favorite things. I asked to speak to the manager, and a good-looking guy came out to meet me. He was one of four sons who ran the restaurant along with their father, who was mostly retired but liked to hang around the bar and give people a hard time. Gene DiMillo was the bar manager who hired me as a bartender, and I liked him a lot because he was funny, sarcastic, and good-looking. Unfortunately, he was married. All the brothers were married, which was too bad because they were all hook-up worthy.

This was a great place to work! It was fun and busy with a great staff of people. Summer in Maine is full of tourists, and if you offer lobster in a floating restaurant that is right on the water, you will be busy all the time. On weekends they would have three bartenders to handle the volume. Of course, being new to the restaurant, I only got to work lunch shifts and occasionally a dinner shift to cover someone. Still, I made enough money to support whatever bills I had at the time and was having a really fun summer working at DiMillo's and living with my sister. The customers were a great mix of people too because there was a combination of tourists from all over and locals who were everything from lobster fishermen to small shop owners, along with people who were actually brave enough to live on a boat all year long. Galivanting around Portland was also fun because there are plenty of great restaurants and bars to hop around in along with ferry rides you can take to visit the little nearby islands.

I worked there for four months before going back to L.A., and I was sorry to leave. Part of me didn't want to go back to L.A. and start looking for a job again when I had one in Portland and was having such a fun time. But knowing winter was looming, I knew I had to get back to L.A. because not only would business drop off significantly at the restaurant, but I wasn't about to spend a winter in Maine. If I wasn't so committed to pursuing my dreams of performing, maybe I would have stayed in Portland and ended up with a very different life, but I still had that desire and felt like L.A. was the place to do that.

The managing brothers and some of my coworkers were equally sad to see me go. I always remember this job with nothing but good feelings and memories. I always go back and visit whenever I'm in Portland.

JOB #22: CAPEZIO ~ SALESPERSON

This job started my L.A. sales career, and let me start by saying I don't love sales, but I happen to be pretty good at it. I only applied for the job because Capezio is a dancewear company, and I always loved Capezio clothes and shoes. The Capezio retail store was on the corner of Yucca and Vine, diagonally across from Capitol Records. I got hired in late 1997 when I got back from Maine. It was only about a mile from where I was living, and I saw a sign that they were hiring one day when I was out for a walk. I went home, got changed, and went back to the store to speak to the manager. The manager's name was Camila, and she was from Cuba but had been in the U.S. for years. We talked and had an easy rapport because I had the sense that Camila was a fun and good-natured person. I filled out the application, and everything seemed very positive. I was feeling like I was about to get hired...until she told me I had to take a drug test.

I guess now would be a good time to tell you I'm a big fan of marijuana and have been for years, so I panicked at the thought of having to take a drug test. I'd never had to before. I immediately called my friend Larry from my Universal job. He now worked at Capitol Drugs, so I told him I needed something to help me pass a drug test. He gave me some kind of tea and told me I had to be sure to drink a gallon of it on an empty stomach an hour before the test. Let me tell you that was not easy and very uncomfortable. Mario, the assistant manager, drove me to the place where I had to pee in a cup and turn it in. I was nervous, but I also had to pee really bad from the gallon of water, so I was literally relieved. The test results took two days, and when they came back negative, Camila called me and offered me the job.

In my first few days, I was becoming familiar with all of the dancewear and footwear and was happy to learn that we got a store discount as an employee. Shortly after I got hired, there was a big sale to get rid of old merchandise, and Camila decided to put a few racks of clothes outside as a little sidewalk sale. Since I was new and still had some training to go through, she put me outside to man the clothes. I was comfortably sitting outside minding my own business and making sure no one ran off with a leotard when I suddenly felt a warm drop of something on my arm. My initial thought was it was starting to rain with those big, warm summer raindrops, even though it rarely rains during the summer in L.A. This thought no sooner ran through my mind when I got hit by a lot of other drops, and I quickly realized it wasn't rain.

I was being pelted with warm drops of bird poop, and a lot of it!

Within seconds, it was all over me. I had bird poop on my arms, in my hair, on my clothes, and some even got on my face! It was horrible. It was like a bunch of pigeons were just waiting on the ledge above to let their explosive diarrhea rain down on a poor, unsuspecting human. I walked into the store with my arms outstretched as poop dripped off of me and tried to stay calm as I approached Camila and told her I had to go home. She couldn't contain her laughter, because after all, it was funny in a disgusting way. If it really is good luck to be pooped on by a bird, I got a whole lotta luck that day. I went home and showered and came back and have not been pooped on by a bird (or anyone else) since then.

Aside from the low pay I got, which was around $9 an hour, and being shat on by a flock of pigeons, it was a good job for me. I was a dancer, and it turned out that I was the only person working in the store who had any dance experience. In addition to my hourly rate, we worked on commission as well. One of the salespeople, whose name was Thomas, was in the habit of aggressively pursuing anyone he thought might be a good sale, regardless of who approached the customer first; the rule was the first person to approach the customer stayed with that sale. This did not sit well with me or other salespeople, so needless to say there were some all-out yelling matches in the store after he would steal a customer. I would have preferred a higher hourly wage rather than working on commission, especially since Thomas was always snaking customers from everyone, but it does incentivize you to work harder when you know you can make extra money. I did okay with commission because I was able to talk to the dancers in a more educated way than the others. Still, I never made close to what Thomas did because I played by the rules.

One interesting thing about this job was that Capezio attracted people from all over the world because you could buy their dance shoes for a lot less money in the U.S. than in other countries. As such, we would get many international customers. It gave me good insight into how other cultures operate when it comes to purchasing goods.

There are certain countries where haggling is how you do business, and I was always surprised when people wanted to haggle on the price like we were some street vendor in Bangladesh. I would patiently explain to them that it doesn't work that way in a retail store in America, and they seemed annoyed by our unwillingness to haggle.

When I got hired, the store was a little hole in the wall. After about a year or so, the store got remodeled and expanded, and it was a lot nicer. They added a small dance floor with mirrors where customers could try on their shoes and actually see and feel what they would be like on a dance floor. There was new shelving installed for the shoes, a big storage area for inventory, and three new dressing rooms with lighted mirrors were added. It was a beautiful improvement compared to the little ratty store we were used to being in. There was a big grand opening and we had dancers from a few studios around the city come by and perform. But the best thing about the grand opening, was that Camila, the manager, was somehow able to secure Fayard Nicholas of the famous Nicholas Brothers as the celebrity guest. If you haven't seen the Nicholas Brothers dance, then go to YouTube right now and watch them. Just incredible! He was old and sweet and small, and I was just thrilled to meet him. Definitely one of the highlights of working there.

What I think would be the most interesting aspect of this job would be the celebrities that came in, and there were several.

I'll start with Debbie Allen. The movie *Fame* was my inspiration for becoming a dancer, so I was pretty excited to hear she was coming into the store. Unfortunately, she would call ahead and ask for the store to close so she could shop privately. I found this kind of obnoxious considering bigger celebrities than her didn't request this. I mean, c'mon, Debbie, you're not Oprah! She would enter the store shortly after her ego, and Camila would fawn over her while Thomas would immediately rush over to her to try and claim her as a sale. It was a beautiful moment when she shunned him and worked directly with Camila because he was so highly bothered by it. I was a bit disappointed that she didn't seem more down-to-earth or approachable because I loved her so much from the movie and TV show where she proclaimed, "You got big dreams. You want fame? Well, fame costs. And right here is where you start paying…in sweat!"

Angelica Huston. She came in wearing really dark sunglasses that she never took off and didn't speak much. She was just cool. I don't remember if she bought anything because she wasn't there for very long, but a worthwhile celebrity sighting.

Renee Zellweger. While dating Jim Carrey after they filmed *Me, Myself, and Irene*, Renee came into Capezio and bought a pair of dance shoes for Jim Carrey. And what I remember is how nice and down-to-earth she seemed when she was checking out. She talked to us and just had a very genuine vibe about her. Obviously, their dancing days were short-lived.

Katie Holmes. Who knew Katie Holmes was into dancing? She came in and bought a pair of jazz shoes from Thomas, who was so busy kissing her ass that neither one of them noticed when she left with just one shoe in the box…and never came back to get the other one. Maybe when she realized she only had one shoe, she gave up her dance dreams for good.

Halle Berry. She came in when she was working on the Dorothy Dandridge movie (side note: Dorothy Dandridge was married to Harold Nicholas, the other Nicholas brother). She was very nice and was commenting on a tap CD when a fan passed by the window and pointed at her. She smiled and waved graciously as opposed to ignoring it, and I thought that was cool of her. Those are the celebrities that I think are the most memorable, but there were quite a few others that came in.

I worked at Capezio for about three years, and then things changed. They brought in a new district manager who no one liked, and it became very corporate. Not being one to appreciate corporate culture, I didn't like the changes that were being made, so it was time to move on. I started looking for a new job and luckily found one that offered me a little more money.

When I left, Capezio owed me two weeks of vacation pay that I didn't use, and they tried not to give it to me. This was the first time I decided to take action against an employer. I was tired of being treated like I was disposable because the only one who ever lost something was me, and although it was my choice to leave this job, I wasn't leaving without what was rightfully mine, and that was vacation money that I had earned.

To be honest, I don't know where I found the information for the Labor Board. The internet was still new, and I didn't even own a computer, so I'm not sure how I managed to do it. Probably the *Yellow Pages*. Remember those? But I got in touch with someone at the Labor Board and filed a claim against Capezio because I knew enough about California labor laws to know that I was owed that money. Someone contacted me, and I gave them all of the information. A hearing was arranged, but it had to be done over the phone because the corporate office for Capezio was in New York.

There I was in the office of the Labor Board in Van Nuys while he called New York and put the executives on speaker phone. He recited the facts that I gave him, and they couldn't deny it because it was the truth. He essentially scolded them and then awarded me twice what they owed me because of the penalty of not paying me when they should have. It was really exciting! This made me believe that workers *do* have rights, and it's important to blow the whistle on employers that are trying to screw employees out of money. It happens every day because people don't know what the laws are or what they are entitled to when it comes to employee rights.

This wouldn't be the last time I took action against an employer; this just gave me the confidence to do it again because there is a lot more to come as far as job troubles and getting fired.

It was a small but interesting group of people who worked there, and I'm happy to say that I'm still in touch with most of them via Facebook. Capezio was definitely one of my longest-running jobs, and I have had very few of those.

JOB #23 ~ TAP DANCE TEACHER, BRAILLE INSTITUTE OF AMERICA

While working at Capezio one day, a woman came in, and after browsing through the dancewear for a few minutes, approached the counter where I was working with one of the other employees. The woman said she was the director of activities at the Braille Institute on Vermont Avenue, which wasn't too far from the store and even closer to my apartment. She said she wanted to know if we could possibly refer her to a teacher who could teach some of the kids at the institute tap dancing.

    I told her I would be interested in the job because I had taught tap dancing (and ballet and jazz) to kids of all ages before moving to L.A. However, they had sight, so this would be a new challenge for them and for me. I let her know that I didn't have experience teaching anyone with any type of disability, but I would be more than happy to help. The woman was so kind and seemed almost relieved that I was willing to take the job. The pay was decent from what I remember, but as much as I always needed money, this time I was also doing it for something more.

    I really loved the idea of teaching the kids tap dancing because knowing how acutely aware blind people's other senses are—being a big fan of Stevie Wonder and knowing what he achieved—I felt really confident I could help these kids and that they would have fun learning how to tap dance!

    It turned out to be a challenge indeed. First of all, if

you have your eyesight, you should be grateful every day for it. It's something we take for granted and the number one sense that we filter our entire world experience through. To be without it is something I can't even imagine. Most of these kids were born without sight, so it was amazing to see how they had already adjusted to life in ways we never have to think about.

The kids I was teaching ranged from about six to ten years old. First, we had to get acquainted, and I always tried to learn the kids' names as quickly as possible. In this case, I had to because I couldn't just look at them when I wanted their attention. I always assured them that the number one thing we were going to have in *my* class was FUN! What I didn't realize was how touchy-feely people without sight can be because they use their feeling sense in ways we use our eyes. When I was meeting them, they gathered around and touched my arms or grabbed my hands and would kind of stroke my arms and hands as they told me their names. It was a little strange at first because I wasn't used to this kind of intimacy, but I quickly understood why they were doing it. Touching for blind people helps them recognize objects, perceive form, shape, and texture, and detect vibrations.

Once we got acquainted, I explained what we would be learning and how we would use our ears and our feet to work together. Keep in mind, I really had no idea what I was doing, so I just did what I thought would be the easiest thing for kids to understand. I did a quick tap dance for them so they could get the idea of how cool it sounds. And tap dancing is *really* cool! It's a dying art, in my opinion.

Then the teaching began. First, I would make the sound with my feet, then I would explain the movement, and then go to each child and physically hold their foot and make the motion with them. It took ten times longer than teaching kids who can see, but it was also ten times more rewarding when they learned how to do it.

The job was only going to last one semester because it was an activity that they were doing on a trial basis. I did the best I could with the kids for a few months, and we put on a little recital for the parents. It didn't consist of too much other than some shuffling, a few basic steps, and some stomping around, but I let them pick the songs, and they had fun, which was all I hoped for. They loved having taps on their shoes and making noise with their feet, but who doesn't?

I'm glad I had that experience because it made me feel like I was giving these kids a new, fun experience and exposing them to a type of dancing that they could learn to do even without sight. It's one of the most rewarding jobs I've had.

Also, at this time, I was very involved with the drummer I had met at B.B. King's a few years before, and we had started writing songs together. After I had been in a few different bands. which were all really fun experiences, I wanted to write and sing my own songs, so he agreed to produce my music. I wrote the lyrics and the melodies, and he did everything else. I loved everything about writing and recording songs. We recorded a whole album of ten songs in his apartment, and I did a lot of the vocals in the bathroom since the sound was better. I cringe a little bit when I hear myself sing, and I love to sing, but I stand by the songs we wrote because I think they're good songs and I would love to hear someone else record them someday. I recently digitized a few and put them online.

The drummer also knew a lot of well-known people in the music industry, like the famous rock photographer Henry Diltz. When it came time to do a photo shoot for the record I finished, the drummer arranged for Henry to shoot the pictures because he was a fan of the drummer, so agreed to do it at a discount! At the time, I had no idea who he was but now knowing what he's accomplished, I feel honored to have had pictures taken by him. He has photographed some of the best music legends…and me!

JOB #24: JACOPO'S ~ MANAGER

Having had so much prior restaurant experience, including being a former manager at Gorky's, I had an easy time getting this job. Of course, I knew the boyfriend of the guy hiring me because we had worked at B.B. King's together, so that helped too. L.A. really is a city about who you know and what referrals you can get.

Jacopo's was a gourmet pizza place with really good pizza and several locations. I was excited to start this job just because I knew I would be able to have free pizza regularly, and if that's not great motivation to go to work, I don't know what is. I worked mostly at the one in Beverly Hills on the corner of Beverly and Santa Monica Boulevard (it's a coffee house now), just a few blocks from the fancy and famous Rodeo Drive. It provided a clear view of the Maseratis, Bentleys, Lamborghinis, and other luxury vehicles that drove by on a regular basis. The location in Beverly Hills was a small spot with about eight tables inside, but the delivery business was the money maker.

This is where I learned what pizza scammers are. For example, a pizza would get delivered, and after some time, the customer would call and say it wasn't good and wanted another pizza. I would tell the customer we would deliver a new one and to return the bad one. The first pizza would come back half-eaten. It used to drive me crazy! I eventually started telling the customers that if the first pizza was missing more than once slice, it was not returnable. These were people with money who lived mostly in Beverly Hills, which made it more aggravating.

The delivery guys were all from various countries, including Russia, Iran, and Brazil. The cooks were Mexican guys from Oaxaca who taught me how to make really good salsa, a necessity in my life. One of the things I've loved about the jobs I've had in L.A. is that you get to meet people from all over the world and hear what it's like to live in those countries and why they love the U.S. It really gives you a different perspective. One of the Brazilian guys, who barely spoke English, gave me a Bossa Nova CD, and he gave it to me because he loved it and wanted to expose me to some of the music of his country, and now I love it too.

I also love that you can meet people, and though you don't speak each other's language, you can find a way to communicate enough when it comes to music and the international language of love!

Just ask that Honduran construction worker I hooked up with.

It's also very interesting to speak with people who had real professions in their home country only to come here and have to deliver pizzas or do other low-paying jobs to survive. I found it to be very humbling, and I have much respect for people who leave bad circumstances, come to this country, and are willing to do those jobs because their governments are even more corrupt than ours. So much so that makes them willing to leave their families and homes to try and have a better life. I have been told on several occasions by immigrants from all over the world that we hit the lottery just by being born in America. I also think about how much better it could be in this country, and as I write this in 2025, I'm not feeling all that lucky to live in the US, but nothing like a perspective check to remind us to focus on the good things.

This was also where I learned the importance of grading restaurants. Every few months, the health department would show up to inspect the cleanliness, the food storage, temperatures, and a long list of other requirements that would end up in being graded an A, B, or C. And trust me when I tell you that you do not want to eat at a restaurant with anything other than an A. If it's below an A, they are doing something wrong!

Anyway, business started to slow down, and guess who started getting shifts cut? That's right. I was the last manager hired, so the first one to lose work. I wasn't totally disappointed because managing restaurants really sucks. Aside from the free food, its long hours, a lot of problem-solving, and too much responsibility for the salary. They eventually started closing different locations because business got so bad, but they also tried to deny me earned vacation pay…and I had to go to the Labor Board again! I didn't get as much from them as Capezio because I hadn't been there as long, but after I got that money, I set that bridge on fire and was back on the job hunt yet *again*.

This was a noteworthy time because my brother and I had been living together for several years, and both of us wanted to get our own places. But every time we wanted to do that, something would happen, like me getting fired. I had to temporarily move into my boyfriend's apartment in Burbank, but luckily, he was on tour, so I didn't have to live *with* him. A few months later, I was able to get my own place, and I also found a new job! The only downer? It was in the Valley. I was now living in North Hollywood, which felt like a step down after living in Hollywood for eleven years, but I couldn't afford Hollywood without a roommate. The Valley had cheaper rent, which is why I spent the next twelve years there!

JOB #25: PRINTING IMPRESSIONS ~ RECEPTIONIST

Printing Impressions was a printing company in North Hollywood, two miles from where I was living.

It wasn't a big company, and I have a vague recollection of most of the people there, but the one person I remember most was named Lenore. I used to call her "Lenore the Whore," not just because it conveniently rhymed but also because she had it in for me from day one! I don't know why she didn't like me, but she definitely didn't, and she happened to be my supervisor. I was hired by the owner of the company, a petite woman with a noticeable mustache, but Lenore was given the job of my supervisor in addition to whatever else she did there. Lenore the Whore was one of those people that lived alone with her cat. Not that there's anything wrong with that since I live alone with my cat, but she might be what you would picture when you think of a "cat lady." When I think of a person who I would describe as *frumpy*, Lenore comes to mind. She wore outdated clothes, her hair was wiry, and she never wore makeup. I think she was very insecure. I also think there are times when an insecure person who has authority over a confident person will flex their "power" as a way to feel better about themselves, so she would find weird ways to enforce her authority. For example, if I wanted to take my lunch hour a little earlier or later than my regular time, she would find a reason to say no.

My job was to answer and direct calls and handle other things like incoming/outgoing mail, putting together any information packets for the salespeople, making coffee, and other basic clerical duties. Easy, right? Of course, it was! I could do a job like that with my eyes closed, especially for the $12 an hour I was making.

This was in the early days of the internet, and I would be online looking something up or reading something when suddenly, Lenore the Whore would sneak up behind me, lean over, and say, "What are you working on?" in a startling, creepy kind of way. I would spin around in my chair and tell her I was looking up something work-related, but I'm pretty sure that's not true. I think she felt it was her job to check up on me but she did it in a way that was weird and suspicious. I didn't like it, so I would give her a little passive-aggressive attitude, and I knew it bugged her that I didn't take her seriously. How could I? I don't respect people who enforce undeserved power.

When I got hired at this job, I already had a vacation planned to go see my family in the summer. When I left to go on vacation, as far as I knew, everything was fine. I had been working there for several months and was fully prepared to return to work after my vacation. It wasn't until I was at the airport on my way back to L.A. that I checked my voicemail to find out that I had been fired! The owner left me this very vague message about how I wasn't needed anymore at the company but didn't give me a valid reason, so my gut told me that Lenore the Whore was behind it. I tried calling, but the owner wouldn't take my call, so I had no choice but to write her a scathing letter. It wasn't even losing the job that bothered me; it was that I had to start looking for another one again! I have job-hunted so many times, and it's exhausting! Job hunting is practically a full-time job in and of itself, especially when you're in desperate survival mode, which I always was.

I have to mention that the loss of all these jobs over the years was partly because (obviously) none of these jobs were what I really wanted to do with my life, so I never cared about losing the job, but I cared about not being able to pay my bills. There were times over the years that I had to borrow money from my family to get by, but it was only when I was absolutely desperate. It was more important to me to support my own dream pursuit than someone paying my way, which is why I always managed to get jobs. But most of them were low paying, and rarely did I even like what I was doing.

JOB #26 ~ SINGING GORILLA

Sometimes little gigs come up to help you get by. As a performer, you have other performer friends who understand being in and out of day jobs and the constant hustle of taking any paying gig or job you can. My friend Mark, who made his living from doing impressions of celebrities at private parties, offered me a gig that he was unable to do.

Or maybe didn't want to do.

This particular gig he offered me was a singing telegram, but it was singing "Happy Birthday" in a gorilla costume. It was in Century City in one of the high-rise buildings at a big financial firm. These were stuffy kind of people who wouldn't ever expect a singing gorilla to show up at their office party. I got to the building, cleared security, and then had to go into the bathroom to change into the gorilla outfit. Once I was in costume, it wasn't like I could casually walk through the doors and ask where the birthday lunch was, so I had to make arrangements with the receptionist and let her know when I was ready. Once she gave me the go-ahead, I ran through the door, burst into the party, and started belting out "Happy Birthday!"

The stunned and confused looks on everyone's faces were priceless, and I was so happy that they couldn't see me because it was an extremely awkward situation. It's not like I was entertaining a bunch of drunk people who would think it's funny and sing along. This was in the middle of the workday with people who were very serious about high finance! No one sang along, just me, the gorilla, singing

"Happy Birthday" to an unappreciative, stuffy executive while his weird coworkers stared at me during their lunch hour. The unenthusiastic, obligatory clapping after I was finished singing may have been the worst part. As soon as I finished the song, I turned around and quickly ran out of sight and into the bathroom to change back into my clothes and get the hell out of there. Thankfully, no one knew I was the gorilla except the receptionist. I slithered out of the building with the most uncomfortable and humiliating $50 I ever made.

JOB #27: IMPORT/EXPORT ~ CLERK/RECEPTIONIST

I hated this job so much that I don't remember the name of the company or what my actual job was, but I can tell you what I *do* remember. The owner was an Arab named Sayed, pronounced Sah-Eed. The VP was a Chinese lady named Catherine Wong, and she had a laugh that you could hear echoing throughout the dingy, rundown hallways of this company. My direct boss was a Russian-Armenian woman named Anait (pronounce it however you want because everyone else did; sometimes it had two syllables and sometimes three) who used to call me "honey." Who calls their employee "honey?"

All I remember is that the company imported and exported things like videotapes. Considering it was in a weird, industrial part of North Hollywood, right around the corner from a strip club, they could have been importing and exporting porn tapes for all I know. It was in an ugly building off Sherman Way. For anyone who knows the Valley, you just have to mention "Sherman Way," and people say, "Eww."

I answered phones, made coffee, and typed up letters for the vice president. I shared a strange office with a Chinese guy named "Anthony." This was not his real name but what he went by. He used to bring his lunch to work every day and eat at his desk. I have a very sensitive sense of smell, and whatever the hell he ate had such a repulsive smell that I used to light incense to try and mask the smell of his food. My supervisor told me I was going to start a fire, so I had to stop lighting it and deal with the smell. How would I start a fire monitoring a stick of burning incense? I'm sure she would have been more supportive if she had to sit in a room with "Anthony."

At this particular job, I was making $10 an hour, which was demeaning enough. Then I went to lunch one day with my brother, who, at the time, was on unemployment because he was in between stunt jobs. I asked him what he was getting per week, and he was collecting more money than my entire paycheck for working forty hours a week and having to smell gross food on the daily. That was even more soul-crushing than me having to work at such a low-level job.

It all started to unravel when I went to lunch one day and noticed a "For Sale" sign on the building when I got back. I asked my supervisor what was going on, and she said, "Honey, we are moving to Torrance." I asked her when, and she said the move was about a month away. I was stunned!

Torrance is a part of L.A. that is way out near LAX. There was no way I was driving every day from North Hollywood to Torrance for the amount of money they were paying me. In rush hour traffic, that would easily be over an hour to get there and even longer on the way home. She told me they wanted me to go with the company and would give me a raise, but it was only a couple of dollars more an hour. That still would not make it worth the drive in my beat-up old truck that surely wouldn't have made it either. I declined the offer, knowing I would have to go job hunting once again, but there was also a sense of relief because this was definitely up there as one of the most wretched jobs I've had.

And I've had quite a few.

To add insult to injury, sadly, after spending close to a year recording my record and another year shopping it around and playing gigs in small clubs around town to promote myself, my producer/boyfriend and I ended our relationship. I knew I couldn't keep on going with the music because I wasn't a self-sustained act who could go around by myself and play a guitar or keyboard and sing my songs. Since I didn't play an instrument, I needed someone to accompany me, but I wasn't musically educated enough to tell them what I needed. I didn't want to start a band; I wanted to sing *my* songs. I was a little bit lost without him, at least musically.

A part of me knew deep down that it was time to change directions if I still wanted to perform. I had been thinking about stand-up for a while because people had told me for years that I should do it, and all I wanted was to be on stage. I had done live performances since I was a teenager and still needed that hit of adrenaline, attention, nausea, and all the other things that I experienced with live performing.

JOB #28: FLY TECK CONSTRUCTION ~ RECEPTIONIST

Fly Teck is a restoration and construction company that started in Glendale and eventually moved to Burbank. This is possibly in the top three of the longest jobs that I've held, which was about three years. I got hired at $12 an hour and eventually moved up to $14, which is what I was making at the end of my employment there. When I first started, it was located on a small side street in a one-floor office building in Glendale. My friend drove me to the interview because my old truck was falling apart and was at the mechanic's being fixed. I was almost late to the interview but made it just in time and was hired on the spot as the new receptionist by Annie, the office manager. The reception desk was right inside the front door, and the whole floor consisted of five small offices and one bathroom for fourteen people. It was a cramped space, and everyone was on top of each other.

Within a week or two of starting the job, they had the company Christmas party, and I brought my brother with me. Being new and not knowing anyone, I didn't want to go alone but wanted to show my enthusiasm for the new job by showing up. This is when I first experienced how the Armenians party. First, they put out an unbelievable amount of food, and their cuisine is heavy on meats like lamb, chicken, and beef that are often kabob style, and other dishes like eggplant, grape leaves, and lavash bread. I like Armenian food and learned to appreciate it more in the time I worked there.

As far as the party, I can't remember if there was a bar or not because they are all about "BYOB."

Be Your Own Bartender.

I was fixated on how they put full bottles of vodka, whiskey, and scotch on every table, and you just helped yourself. This was a mistake as far as I was concerned because I just kept pouring shot after shot, and suddenly, I stood up and realized how hard it hit me. This was after having a brief conversation with one of my new coworkers and telling her that there were some cute guys that I looked forward to meeting. The strange look on her face told me all I needed to know. I was drunk and had to get out of there before it got ugly. I told my brother we had to leave, and we snuck out before anyone could see me. It was the right move. Thankfully my brother drove, and when he dropped me off, I stumbled into my apartment, where I proceeded to puke up all the grape leaves and kabob meat. That was the first of several Armenian celebrations I attended, but the only one where I got that drunk because I learned my lesson about being my own bartender. Luckily no one realized I left, and when I showed up on Monday, nothing was mentioned.

The company handled any kind of water, fire, and earthquake damage and did general construction. It was a busy company, and the phones were constantly ringing. My main job was to answer the phones, but I did other clerical duties like handling the mail, filing, and things like that. I would answer and direct those calls like a pro, but it was not an easy job. I dealt with a lot of irate customers, which made it a very taxing position. This is also where I learned that construction jobs are never done on time.

The two male owners were nice enough (at least superficially), but Annie, the one who interviewed me, was one of the owner's wives. She held the title of CFO, was the acting office manager, and was despised by the entire company. I wasn't there long before I started to notice this. She seemed nice when she hired me, but that quickly changed because she was one of those people who had too much power that she didn't earn and just used that power to make people miserable. She would come into the office and not say hello to anyone and would go as far as to ignore anyone who said "good morning" to her. She yelled at people, she embarrassed employees, she put her nose into every situation, and just spread negative energy throughout the office.

Once I settled into the job, I started becoming friendly with the employees because when you're the first point of contact, you have to learn everyone's name and their position pretty quickly. The emergency crew was made up of about fifteen guys ranging roughly from ages nineteen to forty. A majority of the guys were Latino or Armenian, and they had a hard job dealing with fire and water property damage at all hours of the day and night. I chatted with all of them regularly because I was often the go-between when it came to the customers and the emergency crew and giving them job information over the phone. I enjoyed working with them and had a fun and flirtatious relationship with all of them.

Some of the flirting turned into more than that.

After I had been there for a while, one of the guys on

the crew, who was from Columbia, let me know he had a crush on me. We would flirt regularly, and one day he asked me to go out for a drink, which turned into an affair until he got fired. I don't remember why he got fired, but it was for the best considering we had been trying to keep our situation under wraps. He was married, and I fell for his bullshit story that he had only gotten married for citizenship. He was someone who wanted to have his cake and eat it too, and I fed it to him for a little while until I woke up and told him to get lost. Beware of the married ones, ladies; they are dangerous!

One Halloween, the bosses decided to have a Halloween contest for the employees, and the person with the best costume could win $200. Always needing money, I decided to go for it and try to win the contest. All I needed was a little face paint and something to make me taller to pull off my Grim Reaper costume. I went to a store that sold packing materials and bought two blocks of Styrofoam that I could stand on. I duct-taped my sneakers to the blocks of Styrofoam and instantly became six inches taller. I was covered from head to toe in black and had a long robe that covered my feet so you couldn't tell I was walking on Styrofoam blocks. I walked slowly (obviously) into the party, and everyone was completely baffled as to who this person was because I didn't speak or smile. When I finally revealed myself to everyone's shock and surprise, I was the clear contest winner! The bosses were very impressed with my creative costume, and I happily took the $200.

The contest was one of the few good times I had at

this company, along with the bonds I formed with some of my coworkers over a mutual hatred of our jobs. Most of the employees at this company were not happy. By this point, I had been there for roughly three years, and it was having a bad effect on me; I was stressed out and unhappy. The bosses created a negative environment by micromanaging the employees. Also, because the two male bosses enabled the bad behavior of Annie, who made everyone miserable. One thing I can swear by: the boss or management sets the tone for the company. If a company culture is unpleasant, it's the boss/management who is responsible for that.

Eventually, the offices were moved to a new, big building in Burbank. All the bosses got their own huge office with a bathroom. The top floor was sprawling and filled with cubicles, a lot of which were open for business expansion. The downstairs part of the building had a large parking lot, a lunch area, and a space for the emergency crew to hang out. The reception area was big and spacious, and I had a huge desk that wrapped around, which was a welcome situation after being in the other cramped space for so long. But that was like putting a Band-Aid on a gaping wound.

Despite the new space, I still hated this job, and my hatred was growing by the day! It was a job that I never got a break from because the phones were constantly ringing. I always felt tethered to the phones because everyone was busy, so even if I had to go to the bathroom, I had to tell everyone so that the phones would get answered. Imagine everyone knowing exactly when you were in the bathroom and for how long. It was exhausting, and many times, a coworker would come up to my desk to chat for a minute, but we could never finish a conversation because we were always interrupted by the phones. I dreaded going to work every day and started to look around for a new job. In the meantime, I would just commiserate with some of the other women, who were just as miserable. This was a job where I allowed my attitude to get so bad that something bad was bound to happen.

One day I reached my breaking point. Annie hassled me for being ten minutes late after my lunch break. She called me into her office to point out that this wasn't the first time I had been late coming back from lunch, and I just couldn't hold back anymore. I snapped!

"You know what, Annie? You're the problem at this company! You make everyone miserable because you micro-manage everyone, and you're rude!"

"How dare you!" Annie yelled back. "I do NOT micromanage *anyone,* and I am NOT rude. More importantly, I am tired of your insubordination."

"I don't care! I'm tired of you being mean to everyone, and yes, you *are* rude!"

And then I stormed out. We got so loud that we could be heard outside of the closed office door. Yes, I realize you're not supposed to yell at your boss, but I couldn't take it anymore. I knew I did an excellent job, and to hassle me over an extra ten minutes at lunch, on top of all the other things that piled up over the time I was there, I was unable to keep my mouth shut. You should reward good employees, not punish them. I know there are sticklers who would argue that if you get an hour for lunch, then you have an hour, not an hour and ten minutes. My argument to that would be isn't an extra ten minutes at lunchtime every once in a while worth your employee's happiness and good attitude? Would that be so awful? Not that ten minutes extra lunch time would have changed my attitude toward this job, but little things like that can make a big difference in an employee's attitude.

Needless to say, after I went back to my desk, it wasn't long before one of the owners came up to my desk and said, "We have to let you go." I wasn't even mad; I was relieved. No one should go to work and be miserable every day, but it happens all the time, all across the world. Many of my fellow employees silently applauded my inability to keep quiet since I was essentially speaking for many of us when I yelled at her because I said a lot of what everyone else was thinking. Yes, it cost me another job, but I would rather be out of work than be unhappy every day and allow someone to think that they can treat me poorly because they provide a measly paycheck. As I said before, life is too short for that.

JOB #29: ONE TO ONE MAGAZINE ~ WRITER

While still working at Fly Teck and while perusing Craigslist for another job, I came across an ad that was accepting submissions for opinion articles about music and the dating scene. While I was at work, in between phone calls, I quickly wrote a couple of articles and submitted them. I was shocked when I got a response because I wrote them off the top of my head and didn't take much time to edit them or put any *real* thought into them. Of course, with opinion pieces, that's just what they are. Your opinion. So it's not like you have to do any research or think too hard. It was a new magazine that, of course, is no longer around, or I'm sure I'd still be writing my opinions for them. Anyone who knows me knows I have lots of opinions about lots of things.

I was so excited when they wanted to buy one of the articles I submitted because it was extra money, and it also helped solidify my belief in my writing. When you get paid, you somehow feel validated because now your work has monetary value, so it was rather thrilling for me. I remember the title of the one they bought was *Where Has All the Music Gone?* which was basically a rant about how real musicians and bands have been replaced with pop stars and poseurs. The second article was entitled *Do You Know a Good Meat Market* and it was a double entendre. It was about where single people could meet other single people outside of the typical places like bars and clubs. I got paid $100 for the article. I felt like I could call myself a professional writer since I had sold a piece of work. It's similar to when you get your first $25 for doing an opening comedy set. You feel like legit comedian because you got paid.

When I decided to do stand-up, the first thing I did was start to go around to comedy clubs and check out comedians. Then I rented DVDs of any comedians I could find and bought books on comedy writing. I started writing things down that I thought could work as jokes, and when I got the courage up, I reached out to my friend Mark (who gave me the singing gorilla gig), who had been doing stand-up for years.

"Great! It's about time," he said. "I'll pick you up on Tuesday, we'll go to an open mic, and you'll do three minutes."

I said absolutely not because I wasn't ready, and he told me I would never be ready and needed to pull the Band-Aid off. So, I did.

I performed my first open mic at Hallenbeck's on Cahuenga in North Hollywood. It was fairly disastrous. What was supposed to be a three-minute set turned into what felt like a twenty-minute set because I didn't notice "the light" that they give you to wrap it up. I just kept talking and bombing until finally, the guy literally waved the light right in front of me. When I saw him, I realized that he had been trying to get my attention for a while, and I felt like such an idiot. It's a wonder I ever got on stage again, but I did, and after bombing a lot more times in everything from bowling alleys to strip clubs, I finally started to get better and got to play in the good clubs like the Improv, Laugh Factory, and Comedy Store.

The great thing about bombing is that when you fail so publicly, you really feel like you can do anything after you recover from that. Of all the various types of performing I have done—including dancing, acting, and singing—stand-up has, by far, the biggest payoff. There is nothing that gives you the same kind of high that making a room full of people laugh gives you…unless you're a rock star, I suppose. However, it's exhausting. Still, for the next eight years, I continued the grind of being a stand-up comedian, mostly in Los Angeles. Unfortunately, I still needed day jobs to support myself.

It would be remiss of me not to include this little tidbit: When I first started in stand-up comedy, I did a lot of research. I went to comedy shows, read about comedy writing, watched live performances of as many comedians as I could find, and read a lot of books. One book that I really loved was Joan River's first book, *Enter Talking*. In fact, I loved it so much that after I read it, I tracked down her management company and wrote her a handwritten letter telling her how much I loved the book. The reason I loved it so much was because it is truly a story about how she wouldn't give up her dream. She had so many people tell her she wouldn't make it and that she wasn't good or funny, but she just kept going. Not to mention the fact that she was also one of just a few women performing stand-up in a seriously male-dominated field. She was so brave and ballsy, and I was in such admiration of her unwillingness to give up.

A few months after I sent the letter, I came home, and there was a package in my mailbox. I opened it up, and it was a copy of Joan River's second book, *Still Talking,* and inside it said, "Dear Celeste, I read your letter. I hope this book will interest you even half as much as *Enter Talking.* Love, Joan Rivers." How goddamn cool is that?

JOB #30: HARMON PRODUCTIONS ~ SALES ASSISTANT

There is a classic *Seinfeld* episode where George Costanza is horrified that Jon Favreau, who is playing a clown, doesn't know who Bozo the Clown is, and Favreau's character replies, "You're hung up on some clown from the Sixties, man!" Every time I see that I have to laugh because I worked for Bozo the Clown.

Harmon Productions was owned by Larry Harmon, aka Bozo the Clown. I was hired as a sales assistant to Larry's stepdaughter, who was my boss, and the one sales guy who had such bad halitosis that I still remember it.

Larry would come into the office once in a while and he was always entertaining and in a good mood. Even at eighty years old, he had such a performing presence about him. I immediately liked him because, as a fellow entertainer, I appreciated his outgoing nature, and when I told him I did stand-up comedy, he immediately took interest in me. He would often crack silly jokes, and sometimes he would spontaneously start singing Broadway tunes in a loud and boisterous way. I could tell he genuinely liked people too. He was a fun and festive man, which is what you should expect from a clown, I suppose.

Although he wasn't the original Bozo, he purchased the rights to the character in 1956 and was the person who not just played Bozo but also made him a household name. He was a very smart businessman and was one of the first to franchise a character on TV across the country. He later bought the rights to the characters of Laurel and Hardy as well.

My job as sales assistant was to help my boss with the legal contracts that needed to be set up for the licensing rights, since some of the income (maybe all of it) came from licensing the images of Bozo and Laurel and Hardy to places around the world that wanted to sell items with those images. I would also help the sales guy if he needed anything.

But what my job really ended up being most of the time was a babysitter to my boss's ten-month-old baby. This was also the best part of the job because she would just hand him to me when she had to take calls to keep the baby noise out of her office. For some reason, this baby and I took a liking to each other. Maybe because he was a really cute baby. Honestly, I am not the kind of person who thinks all babies are cute. In fact, I think there are some ugly babies out there, but people think you're mean if you say a baby is ugly. This one was cute and sweet, and he didn't cry a lot, so I had a lot of fun playing with him. This was the kind of baby that *almost* made me want kids. As much as I love babies and find kids to be adorable and funny, I never had the urge to have any myself. When I was growing up, I assumed I would get married and have kids, but that was before I started living my life, and the truth is, I thought long and hard about the responsibility of having kids and decided it wasn't for me. I could barely support myself let alone a child and I wasn't dating men whom I wanted to have kids with so I'm glad I made that choice. And let's face it, cute babies eventually turn into teenagers, and I definitely didn't want any of those!

The baby started to like me so much that he wanted to be with me more than his mom, and this might have had something to do with being "let go" one day. I worked here for less than a year and was told it was because business was down, and that's entirely possible. But I saw her face several times when the baby would cry in her arms and reach for me, and that must have been hard for her. I'm not saying that was the reason, but it's understandable if it was.

That was also the last I saw of Bozo, and sadly he died in 2008, but he certainly left an impression on the world. How many people can say they worked for a clown, let alone Bozo the Clown?

JOB #31: CREATIVE MEDIA ~ RADIO PROMOTIONS/COPYWRITER

I got hired for this job in 2005 and managed to hold on to it until 2008. You might be wondering by now why I couldn't hold onto many of these jobs, and in retrospect, my explanation is that even though I didn't realize it at the time, I was always putting out negative energy about my day jobs. I was always either unhappy with the job itself or the amount of money that I was getting paid, so I think my negativity unconsciously resulted in the perpetual loss of jobs and subsequent financial struggle.

If I only knew then what I know now.

Creative Media Promotions was located in Burbank, and there were only three of us in the whole company: the boss, Bob (who I'll call Big Bob); the younger Bob (who I'll call Young Bob because he was roughly fifteen years younger than Big Bob), and me. Young Bob did a lot of the same things as I did as far as the job, but he also ran around a lot for the boss, who kind of kept him on call. I think Big Bob hired me because I had some sales experience, which is helpful in radio promotions, but I also think he liked the fact that I was a comedian because he had a great sense of humor.

He balanced out the humor with moments of crazy, angry outbursts at Young Bob and me.

Before I knew of his craziness, I was learning about how radio promotions work. Big Bob had a relationship with people at several movie studios, including Fox, Sony, and Lionsgate, to name a few. His company would promote the newly released DVDs on radio stations around the country. For example, when Fox released a season of *24* on DVD (the first show I ever binge-watched), they would ship us thousands of DVDs, and then Young Bob and I would start calling up the radio promotions departments around the country and see if they wanted to give them away on-air during their shows. Once they said yes, we would get to work writing the copy that they would say on air. There's something cool in knowing that your writing, however trivial it may seem, was being read on the airwaves across the country. I liked this part of the job.

Unfortunately, Big Bob was a major perfectionist and would ride us to get more and more stations on board because that would increase the value of the overall promotion and look better to the client. So, if we got fifty stations on board, he wanted seventy-five, and if we got seventy-five, he wanted a hundred. If we didn't get what he wanted, he would yell at us and become slightly abusive. He would often berate Young Bob, who would just look at him and keep his mouth shut.

I didn't have the same type of self-control or fear or whatever made Young Bob keep quiet. If Big Bob started to yell, I yelled back. Young Bob used to say, "Mom and Dad are fighting." At that point, I had worked for too many people that treated their employees like their own personal, verbal punching bag, and I couldn't take it anymore, so I would stand up for myself. One time, not long after I started working there, I had to arrange a pick up from FedEx, and when they didn't show up, he yelled at me as though I had made a mistake. I quickly pointed out, "You're blaming is misdirected, and I don't appreciate it." That time he backed down.

One of the positives about working there was that all three of us were writers and creative types. Big Bob had written and directed his own film and did a decent job with it. Young Bob was obsessed with horror movies and was always working on a new horror script. I was doing comedy full-time at night, and all of us supported each other creatively, which was nice. I would try jokes out on them, and Young Bob would ask me to read some of his work. Big Bob would tell us how everything could be better, whether he was right or wrong. When there wasn't tension in the office over a promotion, the three of us had a good time working together. Big Bob was a generous boss who would take us to lunch on a regular basis, and we hung out at his house a couple of times.

However, as time went on, I was growing increasingly intolerant of Big Bob's outbursts at us. I was also working on an opportunity to do some comedy shows on the East Coast, with the intention of making comedy my full-time job. Young Bob and I were always talking about quitting but never went through with it. Right about this same time, Big Bob freaked out on me about something—I don't remember exactly what it was—and I lost control. I stood up from my desk and confronted him with the same kind of angry words and energy that he was directing at me and remember telling him, "If it were my company, I wouldn't sit around blaming my employees for my own mistakes; I would take responsibility and do it myself." I admit it was kind of out of line, but I had been pushed too far. He told me to go home for the rest of the day, which he had never done before.

The next day I came into work and he was already there, which was rare. He just said to me, "We're finished."

Of course, my first thought was, "This could have been a phone call" so that I didn't have to get ready and come to work. I didn't even respond but just looked at him, collected the few things out of my desk, and walked out. I wasn't happy about this, but by now I had the plan set up to do the East Coast shows, so in my mind, the timing kind of worked out. I did try calling him to calmly talk about it, but he wouldn't talk to me. It's not how I would have preferred to end the situation because, although burning bridges almost seemed like a hobby at this point, I would have liked to stay on good terms. Big Bob also tried to keep me from getting unemployment even though he fired me, but luckily, I was able to prove that I had made an attempt to get my job back by calling him and trying to work things out. I guess the unemployment office called him and asked if this was true because I was able to collect after a few weeks. Once this job ended, I was on unemployment for over a year, and it was rough.

Big Bob and I eventually made up; he asked me to come back, and I did, but it was only temporary. He eventually closed the company and moved to Central America.

I debated on adding this part but realized I had to because it was the start of a transformation in a way that I think is important to mention. Before I got fired from this job, I had also ended a relationship, and it was a painful breakup. We had been in Chicago and got into a huge fight that prompted me to end it. To make matters worse, we got stuck at the airport overnight because of a snowstorm and ended up in separate hotel rooms because I didn't want to spend another minute with him. While crying in the hotel room and flipping around the TV channels, I stumbled onto Larry King, who was interviewing Rhonda Byne, who wrote the book *The Secret*. I know there are a lot of eye rolls about *The Secret* but something she said caught my attention, and I watched the whole interview. What struck me was the message that we are all responsible for creating our circumstances. Something about personal responsibility made so much sense to me. After my experiences up to this point and praying for things to be different, hoping that a god or something else would change things for me wasn't believable anymore. Things weren't getting better. I think it was because I was finally starting to look at all of the unpleasant circumstances that I had been in, whether it was getting fired, always being broke, or not being able to achieve my goals, and I realized the one common denominator in every situation was me! It was that simple. Reading that book was just the beginning of figuring out how to change all of that. It took several years. Personal transformation does not happen quickly.

JOB #32: DONOR SERVICES GROUP ~ TELEPHONE SALES

There's a lot to say about this weird place, but I'll start by saying this was definitely one of the lowest points in my string of low points. This was 2010, I had been in L.A. for twenty years and was feeling like I had hit rock bottom. I knew my unemployment was coming to an end, so I was desperate for a job, which is why I applied.

Of course, the Craigslist ad led you to believe that you had the "potential" to make up to $20 an hour even though the base pay was minimum wage, which I believe at the time was something like $8.50. Totally unlivable wages, especially in a city like Los Angeles. I knew it was a scam, but I wasn't getting any other offers, so I sucked it up and went in for an interview.

The job was telephone sales for Donor Services Group, which was an organization that would be hired by various other organizations to raise funds on their behalf through telesales. For example, the Republican National Committee, the Heritage Foundation, or the Natural Resources Defense Council would be some of the organizations that would use Donor Services Group (DSG). The employees would call people all around the country using a script to get donations, and it was a really strange situation. There was a week of intense training because there was a whole system in place for everything from initiating the phone call to reciting the script to taking credit card numbers over the phone. Can you believe people would actually give their credit card info over the phone to a total stranger? Me either, but they did.

It was set up like a call center with rows of phone stations separated only by a thin divider. The rows were spread around two rooms and probably fifty to eighty people working at one time. More often than not, you worked with different people each shift. There were a few people that I would see regularly, but not enough to form a camaraderie with anyone. A few of these people had been working there for a long time, so they treated each other like co-workers, but to be completely honest, if you worked there for a long time, something was definitely not quite right with your life.

Another notable thing about this job were those "co-workers." The people working there ranged in age from early twenties to their seventies, like the few older folks who needed something to do after retirement. This place was filled with such a wild variety of people that perfectly captured the essence of Hollywood, where it was located. It was right on Sunset Boulevard, and the building used to be the offices for the *LA Weekly*, a local paper that has been around for years. Among the people working there were wannabe odd actors, musicians, writers, etc., along with people who had just gotten out of jail or rehab or other situations that put me face to face with people whose priority was not having all of their front teeth.

I don't judge people like that, but I definitely was concerned about the situation I was in and how I was going to get through it. Nothing about it seemed normal or welcoming. They started you off at twenty-six hours a week, and to get a full forty-hour week, you had to "prove" yourself by getting enough donations for them to add more hours. It was almost impossible to make enough money to live on, even with forty hours a week.

I hated it from day one! The trainer was overly enthusiastic about the job and failed to convey his enthusiasm to me for $8.50 an hour. His name was Kenny, and he said his dream was to be a rapper. He looked completely out of place walking around in a business suit, and more importantly, I thought it was disturbing that he took this strange job so seriously. Kenny would attempt to get us "pumped up" about getting donations as if we were a sports team about to play a big game. He was the type who said he was blessed all the time and thanked God and Jesus a lot. He was homeless at one point and credited Jesus with fixing that for him.

One thing I learned in training is that I would have "sell" (get the donation) for organizations that I vehemently disagreed with, like the kind that didn't support a woman's right to choose. I wasn't comfortable lying to people, which essentially is what I was doing for minimum wage. It made me feel like a complete dirtbag. One day I convinced an old lady to donate money to an organization that I didn't believe in, and when the phone call ended, I went in the bathroom and cried. That's why it was a low point for me. When you're selling your soul for minimum wage and doing something you don't believe in just to pay your bills, you have sunk deep.

No one should have to do that.

One of the rules when calling people was to keep the call short if you determined that you weren't going to get a donation, but one day I started talking to a guy from North Carolina and got involved in a conversation about guns that turned into a twenty-minute phone call without getting a donation. I got in trouble for that, but the guy gave me a new comedy bit after he told me that he couldn't believe that I had never shot a gun. He told me I "needed to go out, get a gun, and just start shootin'." I was on stage that night retelling the story about how I "should just start shootin'" because if that doesn't perfectly describe America's motto, I don't know what does.

For some odd reason, everyone would take their break at the same time, and suddenly a swarm of people would gather in the break room or outside. I would sometimes chat with people during the break, and they all had some strange story as to why they were working there. So many of them just seemed a little strange in some way, which made you wonder if they were here because they couldn't get hired anywhere else. Maybe they thought the same thing about me.

After I had been working there for about a month, I was beyond miserable and looking daily for a new job. This one shift I sat next to two young guys, one from Oklahoma and one from Pittsburgh. Pittsburgh was missing a front tooth. In between calls we would chat, and they both seemed like fun people, so I invited them to my comedy show that night. I was happy when they both showed up. We talked after the show, and I found out exactly how young they were. The younger of the two, the twenty-five-year-old from Oklahoma, who had all his teeth, and who I'll call Lee, proceeded to become an important person in my life. We started out as friends because of work, but things quickly turned romantic. Yes, it was almost a twenty year age difference, but we were having fun, and we really connected.

The best part about meeting him while working at DSG was he was someone who saw these people like I did. To us, everyone there seemed like a weirdo. If we were working different shifts, I would send him a picture of someone wearing a bizarre outfit, like the guy named Moon, who came to work one day dressed in hot pink from head to toe, aside from his leopard headband. Lee made it slightly more tolerable to be there. He also came to L.A. to be a writer so we had that in common along with our physical attraction. He had just gotten to L.A. a few months before so he was just happy to have a job.

Although he didn't hate working there as much as I did, he wanted to make more money, so both of us were looking for new jobs when we weren't dialing for dollars. Thankfully, I only worked at DSG for a total of about two months before I landed a new job, and I left that place and never looked back! Lee was there for a little while after me, but he eventually got out too.

JOB #33: SERVPRO ~ RECEPTIONIST/SALES

Although I was happy to be out of DSG, I knew this new job wasn't going to be all that great for a few reasons. First, I was getting paid $14 an hour, which still wasn't enough to live on in Los Angeles. Not since the seventies, when Jack, Janet, and Chrissy were paying $300 a month for an apartment in Santa Monica. You wouldn't be able to rent a garage for that amount in Santa Monica today. Second, I was answering phones again and working in the restoration business again.

If you're not familiar, Servpro is a brand of fire and water cleanup and restoration franchises across the country. Because I had worked at Fly Teck, I was an easy choice for this job. The owner was an overbearing type who loved guns and tried to act like some type of Armenian mob boss, and his wife, who handled the marketing, was much more down to earth, had a good sense of humor, and was much more likable. The Armenian community is big but small in that, although there's a large population, they all seem to know each other. My new boss knew the people I worked for at Fly Teck, and we shared similar opinions about them.

After I learned the office duties, which included answering the phones, making coffee, and a few other mindless tasks, they wanted me to help market their franchise. In L.A. each franchise has its own section of the city to work in, and they had a nice chunk of downtown. This was great for me! I got out of the office and would walk around to the high rises and peddle Servpro to the building engineers. I was essentially doing outside sales for them and could have helped them grow their franchise if the owner was smart. But instead of allowing me to keep selling their services, he wanted me to learn some kind of estimating software. I'll be the first to admit I do not have a math, engineering, numbers, and measurements kind of brain, and this program was all of that. Not only did I resist learning it, I had a difficult time with it. I was also resentful that he expected me to learn this complicated program for my small wage without offering any commission or bonus. Again, I was resistant and resentful. Not a good combination.

The only bright spot in my life at that point was dating Lee. Working at Servpro coincided with the beginning of the relationship, when it's fun and before you find out how crazy someone is. That helped keep my spirits up once things started to go south at this job, which happened fairly quickly. In fact, it was about three months before the boss and I started to butt heads because he got mad that I was struggling with the software program. I expressed that I could be better utilized doing sales and marketing, but he didn't agree. He also had a sexist vibe and was demanding and condescending. I knew this wasn't going to last, but I wasn't about to quit because I needed the job. However, he got tired of my resistance and "bad attitude," which I couldn't hide, and he fired me. I just couldn't pretend anymore. I had so many bad job experiences by that point that the only way I could fake my level of misery was if I was getting paid a decent wage. But when you're still broke and miserable and someone keeps demanding more without giving more, you eventually run out of the energy to pretend it's okay.

I enjoyed working with his wife but was relieved to get out of there. Yet, here I was again, out of work, unable to collect unemployment, and with no savings. This is when I approached Lee about moving in together and splitting the rent. He was in a strange living situation with some Russian lady he was renting a room from and wanted out so he was enthusiastic about living with me, especially since we were into each other. We agreed it would be temporary, and that lasted eight months before he moved out, and got his own place. But you know the saying, Everything happens for a reason, and getting fired from Servpro led me to a job that helped move my writing career forward.

JOB #34: DEMAND MEDIA ~ FREELANCE WRITER

I was back to looking for work, and by this time, I would look at jobs that were listed in several Craigslist categories, including sales, office/admin, marketing, customer service, and writing, because by now I had experience doing all of it.

Job hunting on Craigslist was always an adventure because along with some legit jobs that were available, I'd have to comb through all the scammy, weird stuff that's listed too. In a city like L.A., there's so much of that! Ads that would say things like "Make $3,000 your first week, no experience" in the sales category. I'm pretty sure you'd have to sell your body or drugs to make that kind of money with no experience. Although I also perused other job sites, like Indeed, I always got more responses from Craigslist. I wish I kept track of the amount of resumes I sent out over the years, and I wish I kept track of all the interviews I went to and didn't get the job. Between submissions and interviews over the years, it must be at least a thousand.

I think now is a good time to mention that of all the things I have pursued artistically, writing is what I did first. From the time I was a kid, maybe around eight or nine, I started writing poems and little story ideas, and it seemed to come easily for me. I think comedy and writing have been the two pursuits that are most natural for me, even though I enjoy singing and dancing a little more. But I've always loved writing and getting my thoughts out of my head and onto a page in front of me where I can make sense of it. I also love storytelling.

Interestingly, writing was the skill my mom always told me I was good at from a very young age. much more so than she ever mentioned my music or dancing talent. Years later, when I learned about the subconscious mind, limiting beliefs, and mental programming, I started to understand why I had more success with writing than my other pursuits.

A year or so before I got this job, I had applied for a writing job for E. Jean Carroll, the longtime writer for *Elle Magazine,* who had a column for many years entitled "Ask E. Jean." At the time, she was hiring someone to work for her in a writing capacity for her website, and part of the hiring process was to offer advice to her readers who would write in with questions. Although I didn't get the job (she told me I was in the top few applicants…but she could have told everyone that), I met some people/writers who were also applying for the position that I am friends with to this day.

One of the women who also applied for the "Ask E. Jean" job told me about another writing job at Demand Media (now Leaf Group). To apply to become a freelance writer, you were required to create a "How To" article about something and submit it. I created my "How To" article by writing "How to Train Your Cat," and I was able to create this without doing any research whatsoever because I had the personal experience of training my two cats that I had for sixteen years.

The first week we arrived in L.A., we went to a

vegetarian restaurant, and there was a sign that said, "free kittens out back." A feral cat had delivered her babies behind the restaurant, and although we knew nothing about cats and were in no position to take care of anything, we decided to take two of them home with us. I ended up with these two cool cats and learned how to train them when I got a new chair that I didn't want to be ruined by their scratching. Writing about that skill is how I got the job.

The article had to be written in a step-by-step/instructible style. This was another writing gig where I didn't spend much time on the submission, but I still managed to get the job. After they reviewed the submission, you would either be accepted or not, and if you were accepted, you were hired as a 1099 independent contractor and would get paid $15 per article, which had to be roughly four hundred to five hundred words. There was never a person that I spoke with on the phone or anyone that I knew was an actual person. It was anonymous copy editors that I emailed back and forth with. I never saw, spoke to, or met a single person.

I was thrilled to get the job at first. That was until I learned how it all worked. First of all, all of the articles had to be written in AP (Associated Press) style, which has particular grammar rules. Some I knew, but some I didn't. There were also certain sites/resources you weren't allowed to use when researching the articles because they weren't considered "valid" resources. This made it really difficult sometimes because depending on what you were writing about, there might not be a lot of resources to begin with. There was a list of titles that the writers chose from to write about. What took me a while to learn was figuring out when the new titles came out, so there was a better pool to choose from. Otherwise you were left with having to write about weird topics like "How to Make a Toboggan," which was an actual title I got stuck with.

Side note: What came up during my research on "How to Make a Toboggan" was the Urban Dictionary's definition of a toboggan. It's a sexual position where a male is poised behind the female at the top of a flight of stairs and proceeds to knock her arms out from underneath her and rides her down the stairs like a toboggan. *That's* what I should have sent to the copy editors!

Unfortunately, the copy editors had the power to reject any of the articles without much explanation, so to keep that from happening, I had to become good at this quickly. That's not to say that I didn't have days where I spent a couple of hours on one article only to have it rejected, and I would cry at the frustration of struggling for peanuts and having no recourse with some of the copy editors who were just dicks sometimes. Luckily, I don't think I had more than five articles rejected during the time I worked for this company. Within a year I wrote about four hundred articles, but there were days when what I was making averaged out to be $5 an hour. It was like boot camp for writers, and as difficult as it was, I'm grateful for the experience because it made me a better writer.

This was also my first experience working from home, and I loved it! The freedom of making my own hours and being self-disciplined was good for me.

While I was still writing for Demand Media, I

continued looking for a job that was steady with more money and maybe even insurance. I hadn't had health insurance for some time. In fact, I have spent more time in my adult life without health insurance than with it. Thankfully I've always been healthy. Health insurance is a total racket, but it's nice to have it living in this country. Sadly, people will stay in jobs they hate *just* for the health insurance. That's enslavement.

By now, I wanted to continue writing as a job, and working for Demand Media is what helped me land one of my future jobs, which involved a lot of writing. Although I don't remember this one with fondness, it was an important job to have and gave me very valuable experience.

Around this time my comedian/actor friend Sardia asked me to be in a web series that she wrote entitled *The Golden Touch*. I played a mom and had a few scenes with a guy that was playing my husband who could not act or remember his lines. We shot it at a beautiful house in Calabasas, and it took several hours to shoot, especially because my scene partner had no memorization skills. But the most notable thing about this shoot was that it enabled me to get my SAG (Screen Actors Guild) card, which is a big accomplishment for most actors because it enables you to get "SAG rates," which translates to higher wages and union protection. After twenty years in Los Angeles and hearing how important getting that card was, it always seemed to elude me. And then I finally was able to get it through this web series. I had no idea it was even possible, but I believe it was 2012 when it was decided that acting in a web series made you eligible for a SAG card. The irony was that I had given up on getting one years before, especially because most of what I did was live performance, not film or TV, and then it dropped into my lap thanks to my friend Sardia.

Getting my SAG card allowed me to book a spot in a sketch on *The Tonight Show* while Jay Leno was still the host. It wasn't a big deal, but still a cool experience to have a dressing room with my name on it. When we rehearsed, Jay was friendly, and of course he was wearing his denim shirt uniform that goes well with his very blue eyes. Any time I got paid for doing anything in entertainment, it felt really good, especially after so much time doing so many jobs I hated. They were the crumbs that kept me going.

Also, since I had read *The Secret*, I started to read more books about manifesting and gratitude. I started writing a gratitude list every day and was trying to make small changes in my thinking and perception of things. Without realizing it right away, things slowly started getting a little better.

JOB #35: INDEPENDENT ADULT TOY SALESPERSON

Always looking for a side hustle, my sister told me that her friend from high school was selling sex toys and making a lot of money. She was selling them by having parties, which were the equivalent to modern-day Tupperware parties. Naturally, I wanted more information about this, so I called her to find out. This would be considered a multi-level marketing situation where you booked a party with one person with the expectation of booking other parties from the first one but with many more fun/funny products. I thought it would be fun and definitely something I could work into my comedy act as well.

I started, advised by my friend, by buying some products from the distributor, like different kinds of vibrators, dildos, lubricants, penis rings, fleshlights (for men's self-pleasure), and other items, and they would set up a virtual "office" to place orders. The products would be drop shipped to the customer. Keep in mind, until I saw the catalog, I had no idea the freaky kind of sex some people are into. Not that I judge, because whatever people do in the bedroom is their business. If I could add to their freaky pleasure and make money at the same time, that was a win-win.

The next step was to book some parties to sell the products. With each party, the idea is that you would book more parties, and that is how you would build your business. This, of course, sounds great in theory, but it never quite works out that way. Keep in mind that both of my friends who got me into the independent candle and sex toy sales were living in suburbia and throwing these parties for housewives who needed reasons to get out of the house and get drunk with friends. The fact that they came home with a nice candle or a dildo is almost unimportant. But living in L.A., people can get candles or sex toys without having to go to a party, so I didn't have the same luck booking parties as they did.

In an attempt to gain more business, I got the bright idea of having my young, hot boyfriend Lee go out and sell them for me. He was very open to trying out the new products as they came in, especially the ones for male pleasure, which made him an experienced salesman who could convince women to have a sex toy party.

And it worked!

I sent him out with some business cards and a list of target places, and he booked some parties using this strategy. What woman wouldn't be open to a cute guy asking them if they'd be interested in an at-home sex toy party? I know he booked a couple of parties when I sent him to the lingerie stores on Hollywood Boulevard. He would approach them and casually ask them if they'd like to have a new, fun experience. This piqued their curiosity, so he would explain the party and that I was the host, and they agreed to do it.

The several parties that I did book were really fun! Explaining (not demonstrating) how sex products work is funny, and there were always women who found out things they didn't know about sex during these parties. I was like their own personal Dr. Ruth. Some people got slightly uncomfortable but were always interested, and then others weren't shy at all! I was a little surprised when one very innocent-looking girl ordered a strap-on and some anal beads! I was happy to educate them on what I knew about the products and how they could make you a happier and more satisfied woman regardless of what kind of sex you're into. I also had a big dildo that had a suction on the bottom of it so you could attach it to a wall or the floor or wherever you wanted to get freaky with it. Once everyone had a few drinks, they would get creative as to where you could suction this thing, like the refrigerator door or the window. This led to lots of laughs!

There was one awkward situation that happened while I was selling these toys. I had an unusually large, brown vibrator (about twelve inches) that was given to me as a joke by my cousin. I had it on my kitchen table one day when I was writing a comedy bit about sex toys. I guess you could say I was using it for inspiration. Just to be clear, I wasn't physically using it! I had forgotten that the cable guy was coming that same day. When he got there, he started working on whatever the problem was and I had my back to him because I was sitting at my desk. When I turned around to ask him what the issue was, I saw him looking in the direction of the kitchen table, and when I turned my head to see what he was looking at, I suddenly remembered the disturbingly large vibrator standing tall and proud in the middle of the table. I started laughing because all I could think was that he must think I was some kind of sex freak for not only having something like that but also displaying it so casually for all to see. I tried to explain that it's not what it seems, that I was a comedy writer and working on a bit, but do you think he believed me? I don't. After signing the work order, as he was about to leave, I said, "Now you have a good story to tell your friends." You're welcome, cable man!

As fun as the parties were, I knew I needed a full-time job because there was too much hustle for too little money, so once I landed the next job, the sex parties fell by the wayside.

JOB #36: MARKET YOUR BUSINESS ~ WRITER/CUSTOMER SERVICE MANAGER

Market Your Business was a start-up company located in a two-bedroom apartment on Hollywood Boulevard. When I went to the interview and I walked up the steps into the apartment, it seemed weird until I saw the setup. It was furnished with tables, chairs, and desks for people to work. It still wasn't an ideal situation by any means, and it definitely looked like a start-up company with everyone on top of each other.

When I got hired, I was still living in the Valley. I interviewed for a writing position that would include writing copy for the website, marketing materials, and writing a blog for one of their products. Market Your Business was the name of the umbrella company for two brands from Italy; one was wooden watches, and the other was a shoe brand. The company was owned by an Italian guy named Dante who had been in the U.S. for a few years and started the company based on his connections in Italy, where the products originated. Dante's English was compromised, and it affected a lot that happened in the office because he had poor communication skills in more ways than one. Despite that, he was a very smart guy, good-looking, and had an engineering degree from some prestigious Italian university.

I interviewed along with a man named Maurice, who was also applying for the job. Dante gave us some weird test as part of the interview process that had nothing to do with anything. I remember it had some kind of problem-solving situation, and Maurice and I had to work on it together to figure out the answer. To give you an idea, it was something like, "You want to cut a birthday cake into eight equal pieces by only making three cuts. How can you accomplish this?" I figured it out, but he hired Maurice. That was my first inkling of his sexist attitude, but within a week or two, Dante called me back and hired me because the company was growing quickly, and maybe he realized that I was a better choice to begin with.

Since I was still living in North Hollywood and was driving my brother's hand-me-down Mazda Miata that was on its last legs and wasn't to be trusted to get me back and forth from the Valley to Hollywood every day, I took the train to work. It was about a three quarters of a mile walk from my apartment to the train station, and after getting off the train in Hollywood, there was close to a mile walk to the office. That was pretty brutal in the L.A. summer heat, only to get to the office where Dante was too cheap to use the air conditioning. Roughly ten people would be working out of this two-bedroom apartment and sweating the whole time. Unpleasant in several ways.

There was an interesting mix of people working there when I started. There were two Swedish women who were sisters, one of whom had been Dante's girlfriend and had started the company with him. Dante's assistant, Javier, was also the accountant and a very flamboyant gay Mexican who I believe was in love with Dante. A Mexican girl named Rosa worked in customer service, and a millennial hipster douchebag named Kyle handled the marketing, along with Maurice, who was the kind of guy that always had a slightly shady side hustle going. I saw him scalping tickets outside of the Hollywood Bowl once, and he also stole some of the wooden watches and sold them on the side. Myself and Maurice were the two oldest people working there, and I was about ten years older than Dante, the boss, who was condescending to everyone.

At first, I was doing nothing but writing. I had to consult with Kyle, the millennial douche, who was also condescending because he was in charge of all the website handling. I was writing copy for the website and blog articles about the shoes. I was also only working part-time at first and continued to write articles for Demand, but at least it offered a bit more stability. As the company grew, I was given more hours, and after several months I was working full-time because my duties expanded to handling shipping and other areas wherever help was needed. The office was completely disorganized because Dante was busy handling overseas issues and manufacturing that was happening in China. He appointed Javier as the office manager, but Javier was the most unorganized person working there. It was often very chaotic. Dante would yell at people and made a couple of the girls cry a few times because he would become abusive like other bosses I worked for. He would argue with the guys, but he would berate the women, and I had a problem with that. However, until it was directed at me, I kept quiet.

After I was working there for a couple of months, they needed another person part-time to work on a temporary project. I was still seeing Lee on and off (mostly off), who was miserable working some delivery job, so I referred him to Dante. He was hired, and now we were working together again. But just like at DSG, having him there as another pair of eyes on this weird situation was great because we were constantly making fun of the bizarre setting we were in. The apartment, the boss, the co-workers, the chaos, and the drama were all very entertaining to us. Once the temp project was done, Dante kept Lee working there in other capacities because there was always more work to do and everyone was behind in their workload. Lee started helping out in customer service with me and learning how to fix the watches.

After several months and after being repeatedly warned about being on social media all day, Dante fired Rosa from her customer service role. She deserved to be fired because she was never on top of her workload and literally would spend hours on Facebook. He fired her at a time when customer service was really busy because the wooden watches, which were the number one selling product, constantly broke. The calls and emails for fixing and replacing the watches were getting excessive. The watches were really cool, but they were made in China, so they were not good quality. With Rosa gone, he needed someone else in customer service right away, and he put me in that position.

When I took over, I would walk into almost a hundred emails of people who needed some type of customer service and would take phone calls from irate customers who were on their second or third broken watch. I would get through every email, handle every phone call, and make it my goal to make an unhappy customer happy again. I had several pages of emails from customers saying that it was the best customer service they had ever received.

I was hired at $15 an hour, and now that I had been there for a while and was managing the customer service department with documentation of the great job I was doing, I approached Dante about a raise. He was very resistant, which is why I made sure that I had written proof that I deserved a raise after whipping the customer service department into shape. He couldn't deny that and gave me the raise I asked for to $18 an hour.

Of course, by now, Dante and I had a couple of run-ins based on how he would be condescending, disrespectful, and/or overly demanding. It's so interesting how some bosses think that it's okay to talk to you a certain way, but if you speak to them in that same way, they get angry. The old "do as I say, not as I do" philosophy never worked with me. I would love to teach bosses how to be better bosses.

About a month after I got the raise, Dante and I had an argument over an email that got sent to a customer. Initially, I forwarded the complaint from the customer to Dante to ask him how he wanted me to handle it. He responded with, "Give him a new watch and get him out of my life." I accidentally didn't delete Dante's response when I responded to the customer and the customer saw what Dante wrote. I had never made a mistake like this before, and needless to say, the customer freaked out! I called the customer, and apologized and said that Dante was just joking, but when Dante realized the mistake I made he freaked out too! Yes, it was my mistake, but his words were the real problem. Still, he considered it all my fault. As I tried to defend myself, everything escalated, and the end result was Dante firing me.

Needless to say, I was really upset because it was an honest, albeit stupid, mistake, and I didn't deserve to be fired. Not to mention that as a 1099 employee, you are not eligible for unemployment, so I was really screwed. I didn't know what to do. Here I was out of work again, with no savings and a car that barely ran, so I had a complete meltdown. I decided it was time to leave L.A. and go back to Philly because I simply couldn't take it anymore. The never-ending struggle and financial instability were just too much by now. I was done!

I started seriously making plans to leave L.A. because my life seemed like it was falling apart. I was talking to my sister, who was living in the Philadelphia area, about coming back and how hard it would be to leave L.A., and she said something I'll never forget.

"Of course it's hard; you're giving up your dreams."

Something about her saying that brought me back to my senses, and I suddenly dug my heels in and thought, "No! I am not letting this city kick my ass and make me leave without getting what I came here for!"

And that quickly, I decided to stay and go back on the hunt for a new job.

When it came time to file my taxes, I owed money because of being a 1099 employee. I had no money, and I started looking into the laws of being an independent contractor. It's important to mention that Dante had everyone working as 1099 independent contractors, and I found out that often employers will do this because it's a way for them to avoid paying taxes. But when you have people in that position, California law states that you are not able to dictate their hours and how or when the job is performed. Dante was dictating all of this and more, and no one knew at the time that what he was doing was illegal.

After I found this out, and before paying any taxes, I called him and told him I needed to set up a meeting with him because I had done some investigating and intended to go to the Labor Board with this information. He agreed to the meeting, and I brought my sister with me as a witness. Dante had Javier sit in on the meeting because he wanted to be sure he understood what I was telling him. Naturally, during the meeting, as I explained that what he was doing was illegal, he got very defensive, and I started to get angry. My sister and Javier intervened, and I agreed to let Dante speak to his lawyer before I did anything. A few days later, Javier called me and said Dante's lawyer advised him to give me the money I was asking for because he was indeed breaking the law. I signed a paper saying that I wouldn't take any action against him or the company after he paid me $6,000.

He paid me the money, and it felt really good to have won that battle. Not only did I need the money, but I felt vindication for someone who was screwing me over and treating his employees badly. A few of the employees called me later to ask how I went about that because Javier and his big mouth told people, but I couldn't tell them based on the agreement I had signed. I told them to do their research and that I couldn't help them, but I believe I did help them in a way. There are so many people that get screwed by their employers and don't even know it because they don't know their rights.

The $6,000 helped me pay my taxes and get by until I got my next job, which was a couple of months later. (Side note: Dante sold the shoe company to Crocs in 2021 and is now worth about $650 million personally).

Over the years, I have cried so many tears of fear and frustration that if I had a dollar for every tear I shed, I wouldn't need to work anymore. But I also think crying releases negative energy, so I encourage people to cry it out. Whenever I would have a good cry, it was like I was able to let go of all the fear and strive on! There were times when I would be struggling and my parents would say things like, "Why don't you just come home? Is it worth all of this struggle? Why don't you go back to school?" I understood the questions because no parent wants to see their adult child unhappy, but I just couldn't give up. I had to keep going because something inside of me wouldn't let me quit no matter how awful it got.

More than once over the years I felt a sense of complete despair that was consuming. I never had any financial stability, and my parents had long before made it clear that they would not help me financially, and they shouldn't have had to at my age. That's what was so humiliating. The feeling of having nowhere to turn on top of feeling like a complete failure is a bad feeling, but I know the one thing that kept me going and gave me any kind of joy in some very dark times was getting on stage.

For the time I was on stage, all my problems would fade away for a little while. Writing comedy helped a lot too. If I was stressed about a job or money or something else, I'd sit down and work on writing jokes. When you are actively working on something that makes you (and hopefully others) laugh, it pulls you out of it and changes the negative energy to something positive. Comedy helped me to keep going.

JOB #37: PORT TEXTILES ~ SALES ASSISTANT

When I went for the interview for yet another job I found on Craigslist, the address turned out to be at a beautiful craftsman-style house in Spaulding Square.

I went from a job in an apartment to a job in a house. Movin' on up!

The difference was the office was in the back of the main house, in what would have been a two-room guest house, and Spaulding Square is a beautiful little section of Hollywood with tree-lined streets and pretty Spanish-style and craftsman homes. It was definitely a step up as far as working in a home office environment. I interviewed with Sam at his kitchen table while his three cats brushed up against my legs.

I knew the interview was going well because Sam and I immediately hit it off. Then he brought me to the guesthouse/office to meet the two women who worked for him: Margaret and Mary. Margaret was originally from Philly, and Mary was a former actress, so I had something in common with both of them. Both women were roughly ten years older than me, and they seemed nice. In fact, everything seemed nice. The office was situated next to the pool, and my desk would be directly facing Sam's desk. Mary and Margaret's desks were in a second room. It was a cramped space overall, but I didn't care about that because I just wanted the job.

The job was to work as one of Sam's three sales assistants. Mary and Margaret were also assistants, but Mary did her own sales as well. Sam was such a good salesman that not only did he need three assistants, but the corporate office, which was located in New Jersey, referred to him as the "Million Dollar Man." He was the number one salesperson in the company and sold millions of dollars' worth of textiles a year, including everything from sheets and towels to window treatments and uniforms.

I was hired at $15 an hour, so I went backward from what I ended up with at Market Your Business, but I didn't have time to be picky. Plus, everything, including the boss, seemed like a better situation than the job before. I would also be able to get insurance, which was nice despite how much I despise insurance companies and think we should collectively revolt against them.

The textile industry is huge, so Sam's area of expertise was selling to nursing homes, assisted living, and senior living facilities. He got in that area of the industry early on and built a successful career. Sam had a very congenial way about him and was instantly likable, which made him good at sales. He also had an accounting degree and was a whiz with numbers, which is a huge skill to have in sales.

After I had been working there for about two weeks, I was driving the ratty Mazda Miata to work and was a couple of miles from the office when smoke started pouring out of the hood of the car. I was stuck in traffic on Sunset Boulevard, so it wasn't easy to pull over, but I finally was able to get into the parking lot of a strip mall. Since this was before Uber, I had to call Sam and ask for a ride to the office. I felt like such a loser. He sent Margaret to pick me up, and she assured me that Sam wasn't bothered by it. I definitely was.

It was moments like this when I would question what the hell had I done with my life. Here I was, forty-four years old, in a beat-up, broken-down car, unable to get to my $15 an hour job. I would think of other women my age with families, houses, and careers and just patted myself on the back for my spectacular life choices. This kind of situation would have rolled off my back when I was younger, but at that point, it was weighing on my back like a ton of bricks. I felt so defeated but had to buck up and keep going because what choice did I have? There was always a part of me that knew things would get better at some point. I had lived through worse by then, so I just kept going regardless of how terrible things seemed. I was just hopeful this job would be better than some of the others.

While the Miata was being patched together, I was able to use Lee's car because he was out of town working on a production gig. He had since moved on to freelance jobs in production and events. This was a blessing because I don't know how I would have gotten to work since my bike had been stolen too. I had a great beach cruiser that I bought on Craigslist for $100 and would sometimes ride it to the train station in North Hollywood, lock it up, and get it on the way home. One day I got off the train only to find it stolen despite the ever-present security guards that paroled the train station. I asked them about it, and they told me, "It happens all the time." Obviously, they weren't good at their jobs.

A portion of the job was fairly easy: taking repeat

orders from current customers and putting them into the computer system, taking new sales orders over the phone, ordering fabric, and things like that. The biggest part of the job was doing cold calls and follow-up calls for Steve. By this point, I had a decent amount of sales experience, and I didn't mind this part of the job. I actually enjoy the personal contact part of sales, and especially closing.

However, there was another part of this job that was hard, and again, it involved numbers and measurements. Sam would sometimes do a complete remodel of a facility, including window treatments, and we would have to understand the measurements. There are a lot of measurements when it comes to hanging things on windows and around hospital beds, and it has to be precise. We would then have to put all the measurements into the computer. If you screwed up the measurements and the order was put in the system wrong, it couldn't be used. Then Sam lost money, and Sam didn't like losing money. Everyone got tense about measurements, and Mary and Margaret always seemed kind of frazzled. They got more frazzled when I asked them for help, so I was always nervous about doing it wrong.

After I had been working there for several months, Sam told me he had seen a car commercial with a great deal for a new economy car. I told him I needed a little bit more money, and he was able to get me a $2 raise from corporate. With my new $17 an hour salary, I was able to lease my first new car in twenty years! I can't tell you how exciting this was. I had been driving a stick shift without air conditioning in L.A. traffic and summer heat for so long that the new Ford Fiesta felt like a Mercedes. It was an automatic with electric windows and air conditioning, and I was beyond happy! To drive without fear was something I hadn't experienced in a very long time, and I was very grateful for Sam's help.

I liked working with Sam because he was a good boss and a fun person to be around. There were many Fridays after work that Margaret and I would join him for cocktails by his pool, and we would share Hollywood gossip.

I worked at this company for almost two years, but I didn't really like the job as a sales assistant. I wanted to make more money and felt that with the right sales opportunity I could. I had enough confidence in myself—stand-up comedy helped with that—and I felt like I had enough sales experience by then. As much as I liked Sam, the job was a mixture of boredom and confusion. Sam had also told me that he thought I had a lot of potential in sales, and I consider him a mentor of mine. I felt like it was time to try having a real sales career, and an opportunity came up that I jumped on, maybe too quickly. When I told Sam about the new job, he was supportive but disappointed, and I felt bad, especially since I had interviewed for it without him knowing. He had been very helpful to me and one of the few really good bosses that I had over the years, but I just felt like I wasn't going anywhere with that company. And even if I had started to get my own accounts, I didn't like what I was doing. I would never be excited to sell sheets and towels. Sam had taught me so much about sales that I felt like I was ready to go out on my own.

While I was working at Port Textiles a stroke of good

luck fell upon me, and I found an apartment with a great deal on rent in my old stomping grounds: Hollywood. I was so excited to move out of the Valley and back into Hollywood because I never felt at home in the Valley. I was just there temporarily, that's if you consider twelve years temporary.

Also, I believed this to be more than luck. I had gotten into more books that expanded on how our thoughts create our circumstances. I started to become more aware of my thoughts and feelings and take responsibility for my circumstances. It still took a little while for things to turn around, but I kept working at it because I was determined to get out of this financial rut. But clearly, things were improving for me. I now had a new car and a new apartment. I started to believe more and more in the power of our thoughts and how we have the ability to change our lives if we know how. It's the knowing "how" that is the tricky part.

JOB #38: ICE BAR ~ OUTSIDE SALES REPRESENTATIVE

For my first outside sales job, Ice Bar seemed like the absolute perfect fit because I wanted to sell something I liked. Alcohol-infused ice cream and popsicles. Since I like alcohol and ice cream, I thought putting them together was brilliant!

This was also another start-up company, and although the base pay was low, I knew I could make more money with the commission. I felt very confident that I could sell this product. I was hired with three other women, and I split the L.A. territory with two of them, while one handled San Diego. I had central L.A., including Hollywood and Beverly Hills, which was perfect for me since I knew the area so well. There were tons of prospects since we were calling on liquor stores, bars, restaurants, and hotels.

The owners of Ice Bar were a husband-and-wife team, Fred and Sharon, who seemed very nice at first. Fred was of Middle Eastern descent. He had a vibe that made me think there was more to him, like he was angry underneath the surface. I had heard him on the phone with someone, and the condescending, irritated tone he used made my radar go up. Sharon was pregnant with her fourth child when we were hired, and she was the type that tried to be hip but instead came off like she was trying too hard with her blue eyeliner and knee-high boots. The sales director, a tall, lanky, and very fake guy named Dustin, did most of the training at the corporate office in Santa Monica.

Starting off, everyone was enthusiastic, and we

trained on the various types of ice creams and product knowledge. All of us were excited to get out and start selling because we all believed it was an easy sale. The products were delicious! There were three types of popsicles—margarita, mojito, and cosmo—and three flavors of ice cream—pink squirrel, brandy alexander, and grasshopper.

As expected, it wasn't a hard sell. When I would sample the products for potential customers, they would immediately like it. Then it was up to me to convince them to carry it, which wasn't difficult considering Ice Bar provided the freezer and the product. All they had to do was find a place to store it. Everything seemed straightforward in the beginning. Once we closed the sale, Ice Bar would deliver a freezer and the products to the business. We would give them an invoice, and under normal business practice, they would typically have thirty days to pay. Not at Ice Bar. Fred wanted payment as soon as the delivery was made, which I found to be strange.

I closed several sales quickly but things started to go sideways almost immediately. First of all, very few of the freezers worked properly and they looked used. A customer would call me and tell me the freezer wasn't getting cold or it was leaking and then I would have to arrange for a new freezer to be delivered. Kind of embarrassing when it's your first go around and you're establishing relationships with your customers. The company comes off as very unprofessional, but it reflects on the sales rep.

I became good friends with one of the other reps,

Krissy, who was working the Valley territory, and we would commiserate often. I found out she was having the same kinds of problems with bad freezers and incomplete orders. We also noticed the prices we would quote customers would differ from what was on the invoice because they would bill the customers for more money than what we told them it would be. Now this was a problem because it looked like a bait-and-switch. My reputation as a salesperson was important to me, and Krissy felt the same way. We weren't about to put our reputations on the line because this company didn't have their shit together.

I knew there was a real problem when I called the office to report a problem and Fred got on the phone and yelled at me.

I said, "Fred, we can't invoice these customers; the freezer is broken!"

Fred responded by yelling, "WE'LL GET THEM A NEW FUCKING FREEZER BUT YOU NEED TO GET THEIR MONEY!"

You probably can tell by now that yelling at me does not go over well, especially when the problem is not my fault. I said, "No, I'm not doing that." And he hung up on me.

Fred also had me go to a restaurant where he had given the owner some products for a party a week or two earlier with an agreement that the owner would pay later. The owner wasn't there when I showed up, and Fred started to treat the situation like he was being screwed over and I was there as his "collector." I explained the situation to the onsite manager, who got on the phone when I called the office, and Fred threatened him about payment. The manager got off the phone and said, "That dude is crazy." It was all very embarrassing because I don't think the owner had any intention of ripping off Fred. After this incident, I knew things were fishy. Things got fishier when it came time to collect commission on sales.

Krissy and I both had closed enough sales to earn several hundred dollars in commission each. When it came time to get paid, suddenly they changed the rules about commission. It went from getting ten percent of the whole order to ten percent of the product that sold at the store, meaning if they were having slow sales, we were getting screwed. We knew this was bullshit, and we weren't about to take it, so both of us pushed back, calling them out and telling them that was *not* the agreement. This caused problems with Fred and Sharon, especially Fred.

One thing I have learned over the years is that some people completely change when it comes to money. Both of them became extremely defensive when confronted with what we agreed upon versus what was happening. Since I had already had a confrontation with Fred over having to collect money, I had a sense (a very familiar sense by now) that I was going to get fired. Fred requested in an email that all of us to come to a meeting in Santa Monica, and I replied by asking if I still had a job. He wouldn't respond to me and then had Dustin call me and tell me to come to the meeting.

"I don't want to drive all the way to Santa Monica just to get fired, so you can tell me over the phone." Dustin replied that he didn't know, which I knew was bullshit, and Fred wouldn't get on the phone with me. That told me all I needed to know, so I didn't go to the meeting. A couple of hours later, Dustin said I was fired because I didn't come to the meeting, and when Krissy found out I got fired, she quit. Meanwhile, the woman in San Diego was gone already because Fred screwed her out of money when he promised to pay for her hotel room during training, and he didn't reimburse her.

One thing I loved about Krissy is that she was every bit as unwilling as I was to get screwed over and wasn't going down without a fight. We both contacted the Labor Board, filed a complaint, and opened a case with them to claim our commission. This is essentially like taking someone to small claims court. We knew this company wasn't on the up and up by now. We also felt it was our responsibility to let the Labor Board know so that companies like this couldn't go around screwing their employees out of money. Sadly, it happens every day.

Krissy and I went to the hearing in Long Beach, and Sharon showed up with their accountant, a very mousey-looking woman, and they both proceeded to lie through their teeth to the judge. Krissy and I were having a difficult time not yelling out "Objection!" every time another lie spilled out of their mouths. After the initial hearing, the judge separated Krissy and me to hear our stories individually, which was great because we knew our stories were consistent since we were telling the truth. Unfortunately, we didn't have the pleasure of hearing the judgement, because the decision wasn't made on the spot.

It had to be "reviewed," but ultimately the result was that Ice Bar had to pay us our commission. In the end, we won the battle. I don't think this job lasted for more than four months and guess who was unemployed again.

I had really been trying to focus on getting a stable day job and making decent money, so I had dramatically decreased my level of performing stand-up. For eight years or so, I was out several nights a week on stage; a combination of bad gigs plus all the major comedy clubs, but the grind was exhausting. I started comedy at thirty-seven, which is late, although I'm a firm believer that it's never too late to start anything. In fact, I started *everything* late. I didn't start dancing until I was fourteen, I didn't start a music career until twenty-seven, and first did stand-up at thirty-seven. I sometimes think that getting such a late start at everything affected reaching the "success" I would have liked, but I also believe we all are on our own trip, and my trip eventually led me back to writing.

The first script I wrote was with Lee, and we wrote a show based on our experience at the call center. It didn't go anywhere, but I learned the format of script writing for TV. Skip to a few years later, and my friend Maureen, who I knew from Philly and who worked in production, moved to L.A. and introduced me to Eileen, whom she had gone to grade school with. Eileen had an idea for a TV sitcom that she wanted help with, so we teamed up and wrote our first script together.

Turns out, it was such a great idea that it was stolen from us.

After spending so much time to get it to where we felt

it was in a good place, we started shopping it around and giving it to people we knew who might have connections. Our mutual friend, Maureen, who introduced us, had a meeting to work on a charity golf tournament with a well-known writer/producer team who already had a hit TV show. As a favor, she brought a hard copy of our script to the meeting with her and left it with the assistant. A week or so later she followed up with the assistant, who said they hadn't read it and were seemingly not interested.

Flash forward to nine months later, Eileen and I started getting emails from friends with links to articles in *Variety* and *Hollywood Reporter* about a new show coming out on FOX by the same team Maureen had left the hard copy script with. The show concept was almost identical to ours, aside from the fact that they switched the genders of the main characters. We couldn't believe what was happening. We knew they had stolen our idea, and we contacted a lawyer to see what recourse we had. The first question he asked was if our script was copyrighted, which it was. We sent a cease-and-desist letter. The problem was that even with the email exchange about the script, there was no proof that they had received the script because it was a hard copy. Unless there was something in their show that was an obvious steal, our hands were tied. Stealing a concept is not that hard to get away with because you can't copyright ideas, so even though we knew they had stolen it, they had done it in a way that they could get away with it. We were crushed!

When their show premiered, we watched every episode to see if there was anything we could outright bust them on for stealing, but there wasn't. Sadly, they took a great concept and ruined it with subpar writing and predictable jokes. It was canceled after one season. Eileen and I spent a few months licking our wounds, and once we bounced back, we moved on and started working on our next script.

JOB #39: UNIVERSITY OF SOUTHERN CALIFORNIA (USC) ~ SALES REP/OUTREACH MANAGER

I was perusing all of the job websites daily looking for a new sales job and had interviewed with a couple of recruiting companies as well. One day I got a call from a recruiter, and she said that they needed someone at the University of Southern California ASAP. It was a telesales position, but without any income (including unemployment), I was in no position to be picky. Plus, even though it was only a temp job, I knew USC would look good on my resume. I did a phone interview first with the woman, Maryellen, who would become my boss. Because I was already vetted through the recruiter, she asked if I could start within two days, and I got the job. It was like a gift had fallen out of the sky. It was also starting at $20 an hour. That's when my faith was renewed. I believed my attitude and staying positive was working!

When I started, the job was on the campus, which is impressive. Maryellen's boss was an old, Harvard dude named Ken, who was head of the department and had about as much personality as a bag of worms. The doctor leading the department was a young woman from India named Natasha. She was very smart, and I got along with her well.

The job was to sell a telehealth program, which was therapy via a computer with a grad student who was studying to become a psychologist or psychotherapist or something along those lines. It was an excellent service to be peddling. Even though it was over the phone, I didn't mind it because when I had the opportunity to tell the prospects about it, it was usually well received. I made calls in a tiny office at the end of a hall and didn't have anyone in the office with me, so it was fairly relaxed, even though I had to make at least fifty calls a day.

The one thing that wasn't relaxing was I felt like my boss hated me most of the time. Maryellen had an aloof vibe, and she seemed anxious and unhappy but was hard to read at the same time. Some days she seemed like she was warming up to me but then she would suddenly get cold and bitchy. I wasn't sure if I was doing something wrong. She was going to be a tough one to crack, but eventually, I did. By now, I was pretty good at disarming someone with humor. Once I started to get results at the job and she seemed fairly happy with my performance, I picked a good time to crack a joke or two, and I got the laugh I had been waiting for. Now I knew things would be okay.

Or so I thought.

About two months into the job, the whole department was moving from the USC campus to a larger office building closer to central downtown L.A. It became a commute struggle because without campus parking, having to park in a lot was $10 per day. I couldn't afford that so the other option was the train. I was living a block from the train station, but once I got off the train downtown, I had a mile walk to the office. To get there by eight a.m. every morning, I had to wake up at five-thirty. I've never been a morning person. I've always thought that morning people should work morning jobs, afternoon people should work afternoon jobs, and night owls work night jobs. I think that makes a lot of sense.

Although I was tired all the time, I was killing it at the job. In addition to the daily phone calls, I was doing presentations about the program all over L.A. County for doctors, executives of large organizations, and governmental agencies. This is where my stand-up experience really helped! I increased the membership of the program by hundred percent within six months and was being treated like an actual employee. Unfortunately, I wasn't an employee, so I wasn't entitled to health insurance, paid sick days, or vacation. By now I felt like I had proven myself. I even had my own office in the new building, so I wanted to ask if I could transition from a temp to a full-time employee. Considering they were trying to grow this area of the department, and I was a critical part of that growth, I didn't see why they wouldn't go for it.

My only hesitation is that I was still getting hot and cold vibes from Maryellen sometimes. But I figured I had nothing to lose by asking to become an employee, so I arranged a meeting with Maryellen. I told her I was interested in something stable and asked if would they consider making me permanent. Naturally, she said she would have to discuss it with Ken because he would ultimately make the decision, but I knew she had a lot of influence. He didn't really pay much attention to what I was doing. He said about five words to me the whole time I worked there.

The next day Maryellen met with Ken and then came into my office with a look like she was getting ready to deliver bad news.

She was.

She said that it wasn't in the budget to add a full-time employee and said if I needed to start looking for a new job, she understood and would write me a great recommendation, which she did. I was bummed because I was so tired of all the job hopping and instability, and I knew working for a school like USC would provide some much-needed security. Knowing that this temp position was now coming to an end sooner than later, I immediately started putting out resumes for other jobs.

Then, things got weird.

I had done a presentation in San Diego, and when I submitted my expense report, Maryellen disputed the trip expenses and didn't want to reimburse me the full amount. Considering that I wasn't a full-time employee and needed the money, I argued my side of it. When I told her that there was no reason for her to dispute it because I wasn't lying, she got really angry. She came into my office on a Wednesday and told me my last day was on Friday, as in two days later. I was stunned and knew it was because I had pissed her off, but it wasn't fair to give me two days' notice.

"I know it's hard," she said, whatever the hell that meant.

I told her I wanted to speak to Ken about it, and when I went into his office later that day, I explained to him that if I were the one making the decision to leave, I would have given him two weeks' notice. That is the professional and courteous thing to do, and I would have expected the same professional courtesy considering the excellent job I was doing. I left his office and later that day, he told Maryellen to give me two weeks more at the job. It was an awkward two weeks as I avoided everyone as best I could by staying in my office and only talking to Maryellen when I had to.

Again, I was frantically looking for another job but had gotten myself into a new mindset of staying positive and trusting that something better would come along. This was quite a challenge after all the time and terrible jobs that I had up to this point, but I was determined to stay focused. Every day I spent some time reading segments on a website that was all about the power of our minds, gratitude, abundance, and things like that. It helped keep my head in a good place, considering I was back to the drawing board for the hundredth time.

But I believe my mental diligence paid off because I was finished at USC in November, and by December I had landed my next job. It's important to note that after leaving USC, Maryellen called me back twice to work there with a salary increase of more than what I had initially asked for. But not long after that, I was making almost double what she offered.

JOB #40: MAMA TRUE BBQ ~ CATERING BARTENDER

Not long after I moved back to Hollywood, and while still working at USC, I found out that a woman my sister went to high school with lived in the same apartment building. Her brother owned Mama True BBQ, and she was the catering manager. During their busy season, she needed extra bartenders, and now that I was living in the building, she could easily hire me. I was happy to make some extra money.

I had worked three events with this company, and I noticed that Molly was not a person who handled stress well. I'll be the first to say that events, catering, restaurants, and anything in the service and/or hospitality industry is always stressful. Some people can handle it, and others can't. She couldn't. Molly would snap at people and yell if someone made a mistake and went way over the top about the smallest things. No one liked working with her because her energy was so frantic, but everyone did it for the money. She had a thing about tipping, meaning that she never would allow tip jars for the bartenders because she thought it looked tacky. At upscale events, I agree. However, sometimes people tip you whether you have a tip jar or not, and no bartender is about to refuse a tip.

I was working at an outdoor summer wedding in Ojai, and it was hot. Molly had been running around all day like an angry, headless chicken while the bartenders and servers carried all of the equipment through the dusty ranch grounds to set up for the reception. Once the ceremony ended, the guests came outside, where the bar was set up, and things started getting busy. Everything was going well; the crowd was young and friendly and started leaving tips.

Since I was working with another bartender, we knew to split the tips at the end of the night, so we had to put them somewhere while we were working. All we had were glasses, so we used a type of beer glass to put the tips in, and I put the glass mostly out of sight behind a vase that was on the bar because there was nothing behind the bar to put the glass on. Molly was roaming throughout the party looking for trouble, and she eventually came back behind the bar. She took one look at the tip glass and lost her mind! She directed this tirade at me, assuming it was my doing because the other guy had worked with them a lot more than I had.

She started yelling, but the guests couldn't hear her over the DJ's music. "What did I tell you about tip jars? How dare you have that out!" I started to defend myself when she took a step toward me, put her finger in my face, and said, "Now you listen to me…"

I took a step back and said, "Whoa!" because she was a few seconds away from me breaking her finger. I put the tip glass on the ground, and she walked away. The other bartender looked at me in shock and muttered about what a bitch she was. The rest of the evening I was fuming but had to put on a happy face for the guests while I collected more tips.

To make matters worse, the catering staff all drove in a van together, so I had to be in the same vehicle with this psycho for an hour and half drive back to Hollywood and then deal with the awkwardness of getting out of the van together and then the walking back to the same building. I wasn't about to wait and walk with her after the finger incident. Naturally, I got out of the van as fast as I could and just walked off while she said goodbyes to the staff. Needless to say, that was my last time working with her. Thankfully, she moved out of the building not too long after that and eventually, I was driven out of the building by the woman who moved in next to me.

By now, I was in my mid-forties and decided it was time to stop focusing on my starving artist dream life and get serious about making money. I also decided to make my next day job my priority because making my performing career my priority had made me suffer financially for so many years, and I was ready to change that. On one hand, this was an easy decision because I was tired of the financial struggle, but there was also a sense of letting go of something that I loved so much and had focused on for so long but that still hadn't come to fruition, so I decided to be practical for once in my life. I made a conscious decision to focus on a sales career since I knew I was good at it and wasn't getting any younger. Once I made this decision, things started to turn around quickly. I wasn't giving up my creative pursuits, just putting them on the back burner for a while.

I had also gotten in deeper with the things I had been reading about our subconscious mind and creating better circumstances for ourselves. One continued message through all the reading I was doing was the power of gratitude, and it turns out that is hundred percent true. Practicing and feeling gratitude is absolutely life-changing if you commit to focusing on being grateful as often as you can until it becomes a habit. I continued to read books and research on how to become more aware of your thoughts and how to break old habitual thinking patterns. Doing all of this made me feel better and happier. It takes a lot of practice, but practicing feeling grateful isn't laborious at all and makes you feel a lot better. I was finally consciously focusing less on fear and what I was lacking and focusing more on all that I had. As a result, things changed around financially in a very big way.

JOB #41: BCS RECYCLING ~ OUTSIDE SALES REP

Having USC on my resume combined with my prior sales experience definitely helped me get this job as a sales rep selling the services of the largest electronic recycler in California.

What almost kept me from getting it was a drug test!

After the initial interview, which was held in a hotel conference room near LAX with a guy named John Tucker, I was flown up to Stockton, California, to the corporate offices to meet with the president and VP of Sales. All went well, and I was offered the job contingent on a background check and drug test. Let the panic begin! I hadn't had to take a drug test since my Capezio days roughly fifteen years before. This was in December, right before Christmas, and I wouldn't be drug tested until after the new year. I immediately stopped smoking weed, started drinking more water, and taking niacin, hoping that three weeks of this would be enough to clear my system.

A few days before I was to go up north for training, I took an at-home drug test and failed. Now I was really panicked.

During training, I could barely concentrate. All I could think about was the impending drug test. I just wanted to get it over with and was crossing my fingers and hoping for the best. I was told that I would be drug tested the next day by HR and it would be an oral drug test. I wasn't familiar with this kind, so I immediately started googling oral drug tests and found out that they can only detect marijuana through an oral test within twenty-four hours of use. I was somewhat relieved but still not out of the woods. For a full day and a half before the drug test, I had knots in my stomach, and my palms were sweating because I thought if I lost this job because of smoking pot, I was going to be really pissed at myself. And pissed at the stupid company for having a stupid drug test.

We completed our first day of training, and the next day the drug test was the first thing I had to do. They took a mouth swab, and I sat there nervously waiting for the results. Several panic-stricken minutes later, the head of HR came around the corner with a grim look on her face. My blood ran cold. She walked toward me and said, "We are officially offering you the job." I let out a huge sigh of relief and then immediately wondered if that seemed suspicious. Nevertheless, I was over the moon! I would now be making a base salary of $50,000 a year plus commission. Plus health benefits and working from home, which gave me a lot of freedom.

During my first three months in the "ramp up" phase, as they call it in sales, I was also getting an extra $2,000 a month until I built up my territory enough to make commission on my own. This was more money than I had in my entire adult life, and let me tell you, I felt like a millionaire! I was able to move into a better apartment, I could pay my bills easily, and I was able to go out to dinner and go on trips. This was only the second time in my life in L.A. where I wasn't stressed financially (the first being when I was working in radio promotion). If anyone says, "Money can't buy you happiness," they are wrong! I mean, maybe it doesn't buy you complete internal happiness, but it alleviates a lot of stress. Also, I was fully convinced by now that all of my internal work was truly paying off. I had continued to learn about the power of our minds and practice gratitude, and the results were amazing to me.

By my fifth month, I was doing pretty well in getting new accounts and feeling more confident. One day, I got a call from a guy who was looking for a new recycler to handle his e-waste events. This potential new customer named Kurt was out of his mind, but I didn't know that yet. I was just excited about this big prospect. My boss John, whom I initially interviewed with, came down for the meeting. After discussing pricing, logistics, and other details, we were able to close the sale. I was thrilled, but that's because I didn't know yet that Kurt was going to start calling me ten times a day. The good news is that he was bringing in up to five trailers of materials on a weekend, and I got commission by the pound. Unfortunately, almost immediately, Kurt started to become a problem. He would call me on the weekends, and if I didn't answer, he would immediately call back until I picked up, and then the conversation would go something like this:

"Hi Celeste, can you see if we can get another trailer?"

"No, Kurt, the offices are closed, and that has to be arranged in advance."

"Then I'm gonna have to close the event early."

"Okay, if that's what you have to do," I said.

He would call a half an hour later, "Hi Celeste, we're running low on pallets, can you some more and get them at a better price?"

"Kurt, I can't do anything on the weekends, and we can't change the price of the pallets."

Then he would threaten to go to a different recycler. If Kurt called me and I didn't answer, he would then call my boss. He pissed off everyone who worked in shipping and logistics. Even the people he hired to work his events didn't like him. But by now, he was one of my bigger accounts, and so my boss told me to put up with him. I eventually started setting some boundaries, and Kurt didn't like that. He threw me under the bus several times to my boss. Meanwhile, like in any industry, people get reputations, and word gets around about things. It turns out, Kurt had worked with most of the recyclers in SoCal before he found me, but they wouldn't work with him anymore. Some of my customers knew about him and told me stories about what a shyster he was. I googled him and found out he had been in jail for fraud back in 1996. It turns out that he was going around with a javelin in his hand asking for donations for the Olympics that year! I suppose the javelin really sold it for him.

After several months of his craziness, his e-waste events slowed down, and he wasn't bringing in as much business, so they made him a "house account." That meant I wasn't getting the commission anymore, but my boss had to handle him. Kurt eventually drove my boss crazy enough that they told him BCS couldn't work with him anymore. That was slightly satisfying.

Meanwhile, I had also closed one of the biggest accounts in recycling at the time, which was the Salvation

Army. A few months later, at the annual sales meeting, I won a trophy for "Big Catch of the Year" and was told that no sales rep had achieved the numbers their first year as I had. Everyone was seemingly very impressed with my performance, including upper management.

Everything was going well for a while, and everyone seemed happy until things started to change. My boss always left me alone and didn't question anything I did because I was bringing in sales and also sending a weekly report of my activity. Suddenly, he started to give me directions to change the pricing on customers that was different than the agreement they signed when they came on. I believe these directions were coming directly from the top because there were looming financial troubles, but no one knew that yet. The old bait-and-switch never goes over well, so you can imagine how this started to cause problems. As much as some of my customers liked working with me, and I told them these decisions were over my head, they realized that they could get more money and less nickel and diming from some of the competitors. I had no control over this and started losing customers.

I kept working and hunting for new customers when one day, about a month later, I got an email from my boss saying that he was concerned about my performance, that I needed to increase my numbers, and this should serve as a first warning. I was floored considering that I was still pulling in good volume because of Salvation Army. Even though I had lost some smaller accounts, I assumed he knew that wasn't my fault; rather, it was a direct result of the increase in pricing that I had no control over. I tried calling my boss to discuss the email and to find out where this was coming from, and he wouldn't take my call. This signaled a red flag to me, so I decided I should start documenting the communication in email. I sent back an email defending why I had lost sales due to the pricing and stating that I was confused as to where this "warning" was coming from. His response to my email was, "There should be no confusion. Your job is to bring in new business, and if you fail to do so, you will receive another warning that could lead to termination." Again, I was shocked. Up until this, we had always had an easy rapport and joked with each other. When the tone of his response was so cold and defensive, I had a feeling something else was going on, but I had no idea what. I tried to defend my position, but his responses started giving me the old familiar feeling that I had somehow fallen from grace and I was being put on the chopping block. I had no idea why, and this is after I had been there a year and ten months.

Things heated up as my boss really started putting pressure on me. He suddenly started giving me a monthly quota for securing new accounts. When I kept meeting the quotas, he then changed the quota from the number of new accounts I had to secure to a certain amount of volume in pounds. For example, if he said I needed to get three new accounts and I got them, he would suddenly change the quota from three new accounts to getting fifty thousand pounds of material. I had no control over what the volume of the account would be. He was clearly trying to change the rules and make it harder. Then he hired a new guy and put him in my territory!

Now I knew he was planning to get me out but had no idea why or what I had done. He gave me some bullshit excuse for hiring a person for my territory, but I knew something was up, and for the next several months I worked every day with a pit in my stomach knowing that he was setting me up for a fall. It was horrible, especially when I found out that my boss was sending the new guy into some of my accounts, and when I went over his head to upper management, I got no help.

The only possible reason I could guess as to why he seemed to turn on me was because of a conversation we had right before things got strange, when he told me to start loading the CRM with a lot of prospects that weren't necessarily viable. When I told him that I would prefer to qualify the prospects first, he demanded that I "just fill the pipeline." Instead of being able to make sure they were prospects that would be worth my time, he wanted me to put in anyone so it looked like I was doing more work. This made no sense to me. It was like busy work and I pushed back a little bit and questioned him about it, but I eventually did it. I think his bosses, upper management, and the owners were putting heat on him, so he just wanted me to make it look like *he* was doing his job by having me put in new, bullshit prospects. He was lazy, and I knew that.

By now I was documenting all communication to and from my boss and saving it to a file. I also had Joe, the warehouse guy, who had inside info, letting me know of any shady activity. He told me that BCS was not paying their vendors, and some of them wouldn't work with the company anymore. There were a lot of strange things going on while I was fighting to keep my job and my head above water. After about six months of all of the drama between myself, my boss, the new guy, and trying to get upper management involved, I finally got the email from my boss asking me to meet him and the VP of Sales at a Denny's in Burbank and that I should bring my computer. He gave me some vague reason for the meeting, but he didn't know that I am not the type that goes down without a fight, so I was prepared for whatever was to come.

I walked into the Denny's, and my boss was coiled up in the booth like the snake that he was. The VP of Sales was across from him. I sat down next to my boss, who didn't say a word, while the VP of Sales told me that "it wasn't good news." He said they were letting me go, and I just looked at both of them but didn't say anything. The VP put some papers in front of me. One of them was an offer of $10,000 in addition to my vacation pay and commission. It was essentially an offer of $10,000 to not sue them because they clearly knew they had no real grounds for firing me. I said no to the $10,000 but would take $20,000 of their hush money. He said no, to which I replied that this was wrongful termination. He said, "Do whatever you have to do."

So, I did.

Although the $10,000 was tempting and part of me just wanted to take the money and run, I knew it wasn't enough for what they were doing to me, which was wrongfully taking away my livelihood. Based on my knowledge from past experiences, I knew I had a good case for wrongful termination.

After I got fired, I looked into some wrongful termination lawyers. I found a reputable one in Beverly Hills, who after hearing my side of it and seeing the documentation I had, agreed to take the case. He would only get paid if they won the case, and they believed they could win. After giving all of my testimony to the lawyer, he said about my boss, "It sounds like someone started to hold him accountable," which was the same conclusion of my friends and family when I told them the details of what happened.

Meanwhile, Joe at the warehouse was giving me intel on the declining state of the company. He said there were financial problems, and they were getting worse as vendors were starting to sue them for non-payment. This was a concern, as my lawyer's initial request was for $350,000, which I thought was high, but I was letting him do his job. I let my lawyer know what I was hearing from Joe. BCS's lawyer responded to my lawyer's request and documentation, saying they would negotiate a "reasonable" settlement. All of the back and forth between lawyers takes a lot longer than I expected, and during all of these months, Joe was giving me information. He told me that BCS was preparing to file for bankruptcy! This made me really nervous, so I immediately called my lawyer and told him the news so he would know to act fast because things were looking a lot more uncertain. I was worried that if they filed for bankruptcy, I wouldn't get anything, which meant he wouldn't either.

For some reason, the months dragged on, and I wasn't hearing anything from my lawyer until one day he said that the bankruptcy had been filed and there wasn't much more that could be done. I believe my lawyer waited too long from the time I contacted him. He told me they would try to get some money from filing some other thing with the court, but in the end, BCS got off with bankruptcy, and I got zip! They screwed over so many people in that company along with a lot of vendors, and meanwhile, the owners had been stashing cash and transferring assets the whole time. Very dirty people in a dirty industry. I think it took a year and a half for the whole thing to be over, and although I got nothing and was very disappointed because they had been so dirty, I was happy to be done with it and move on. I still hope karma gave my old prick boss a good kick to his tiny testicles.

JOB #42: THE VALLEY RECYCLES ~ SALES REP (FREELANCE)

Within days of getting fired from BCS, I started getting calls from my former customers to come work for them. The Valley Recycles was a small recycling business in Van Nuys, and I had been trying to get their business while working with BCS. During one of my visits, Eli, the owner, said he would love to have a rep like me working for him. I kept that in mind when I knew I was on the chopping block at BCS. I called him after I got fired, and he said that word had already gotten around and he would be interested in speaking with me. After discussing the expectations and salary, we agreed to a freelance type of position, and he would pay me a small monthly fee plus some commission after business started coming in. I agreed to it because I was working for another recycler in a different capacity (next chapter) and was getting slightly more per month, so I planned to split the week working part-time for one and part-time for the other since both were paying me part-time money.

I quickly started getting prospects, but as with most types of sales, it can take a while before you see the results of building relationships and establishing trust with your prospects because all of that takes time. I wanted to reassure him of that so he knew that I was "earning" my money.

One thing I don't like to do is ask for money, and if we have an agreement that you pay me at a particular time, then I expect to be paid without having to ask for it. I had to ask Eli for payment every time. He also had some unreasonable expectations about my getting business despite filling out a weekly spreadsheet for him so he knew the prospects I was visiting and the stage of the potential sale. By the third month I was working for Eli, I had some strong prospects that I knew I could close soon. I sent Eli an email regarding getting paid, and he didn't respond. I called the office and left a message with the receptionist, and he didn't call me back. I sent another email asking if there was a problem and what the hold up of payment was and he didn't answer it. At this point, I got that old, familiar feeling of getting screwed over again, and I was right. He didn't even have the balls to respond to me and to this day, still owes me $1,000. It wasn't worth going after such a small amount, so I moved on with my life. I trusted that karma would take care of that in some way, as I hoped it did in many of the situations where I got burned.

JOB #43: SAFE ASSET RETURN ~ SALES REP (FREELANCE)

Within days of getting fired from BCS, I also got a call from a former fellow sales rep named Gary who had quit BCS. Gary told me that he found an investor for his new company, Safe Asset Return. He asked me if I wanted to join him as the local L.A. rep since he lived eighty miles outside of the city. I let Gary know that I couldn't work strictly on commission, so after meeting with the investor, he agreed to pay me a small monthly salary, and I got to work.

One day I was going through a list I had created of prospects and happened to cold call the Hospital Association of Southern California (HASC). The next day I got a call back from a woman named Katie who wanted to know more about the company. We set up a meeting, which was exciting after finding out that HASC was like an umbrella association for all the hospitals in Southern California. That meant potentially big money! Katie told us that she was new at her job and one of her duties was bringing in new vendors and revenue streams. When Gary explained the kind of money that is in hospital recycling, she was all ears. Katie took the information back to her supervisor, and then we had to wait and hope that they wanted to set up a meeting.

What initially seemed like a deal that would happen relatively quickly started to turn into a couple of months, partly because Gary was supposedly getting everything set up. But when I would ask him what the latest was on getting a meeting with her supervisors, he made it seem like Katie was dragging her feet. Knowing that I was on shaky ground financially because I didn't know how long the investor was going to continue to pay me, I kept on top of Gary so we could get this deal done. After about a month of excuses, I started to feel a little suspicious, so I reached out directly to Katie to see what she had to say. I got a similar response from her, which was a bit vague but still assured me that there was interest in making this deal happen. However, I was getting a bad feeling in my gut, an all too familiar one, that something bad was going to happen. In the meantime, I was looking for other business and when I would check in with Gary about the deal, there would always be an excuse.

Then Gary said he was meeting with his investor because he wanted some more money for logistics and transportation and also wanted to get the investor excited about this deal. By now, I was in a very precarious position because I had lost the money I was making with the other recycler as a freelance rep and couldn't afford to live just on what Gary's investor was paying me. When I explained that I had lost my other source of income, Gary said he was going to ask the investor for a pay increase for me, at least until we started making money from this deal. He said he felt confident he would be able to get me more money.

What happened instead is that the investor said he was finished investing in Gary altogether, meaning my salary too! When Gary delivered this news, he said he was completely shocked. He said the investor would pay me for that month, and that was that. I believe that he lost faith more in Gary than in me because I found out shortly after this happened what an idiot Gary was.

I told Gary that I had to look for other jobs but still planned on doing this deal that I brought to the table. So imagine my surprise when I found out a couple of weeks later that there had already been a meeting scheduled with Katie, her supervisors, and the rest of the team. The only reason I found out about it was because one of her supervisors, when asking for something about the meeting, happened to cc me on the email. When I realized that both Gary and Katie had, for some reason, tried to cut me out, I was furious!

I called Gary and did not hold back in telling him what a snake he was!

"I can't believe you would stoop so low as to cut me out of a deal that I brought to you," I said. "I thought you were a Christian (only because he said it proudly several times). You are just a huge disappointment as a human being."

He immediately admitted his wrongdoing and said, "You're a good person, and I shouldn't have done that."

I was equally disgusted by Katie considering I brought this deal to the table for both of them, and here they were trying to do a back door deal without me. I was furious but hurt too, especially after the other recycler had screwed me over. I felt horrible on so many levels. But never being one to give up easily, I told him I would be at that meeting, so be prepared to have me there. When I got there, I made Katie uncomfortable, and seeing her squirm made me kind of happy.

After the meeting, I gave Katie a polite, firm handshake, and Gary and I left together. I told him I thought it went well, even though I didn't even care anymore. I didn't want to do a deal with them. Gary was dirty, Katie was dirty, and I was so disgusted by what happened that I lost all interest in working with either one of them. I told Gary to let me know if the deal closed, and he assured me that when it did, I would get my percentage of everything. As if I would have believed anything that came out of his mouth.

It's interesting what money and desperation do to people because I know he was desperate, and I had been there before. I do believe he felt bad about what he did, but then again, I think he only felt bad because he got caught. I never found out what happened with the deal and didn't care to know. I moved on and decided it was time to get out of the dirty recycling business.

There was one good thing that came out of working for Gary. Since he had joined the Hollywood Chamber of Commerce, I was able to attend networking events and other events that they put on. One of the events was to honor members of the community who had given back to the city of Los Angeles, and one of the people they were awarding was Steven Levitan, the creator of *Modern Family*. He was considered a major contributor since he filmed a hit TV show in Los Angeles. I was at the ceremony and waited until almost everyone had said their hellos to him. He was about to leave the room, and I approached him and told him I was a writer and a big fan of the show. He instantly warmed up to me, and so I asked him for a selfie, which he graciously gave me. That's the best thing that came from working with Gary the Snake.

After this debacle and my freelance jobs bit the dust, I was in a really precarious financial position. Although I managed to save some money while working for BCS, I quickly blew through that when I went from making over $100,000 a year to making $25,000 the next. This is when I had to dig my heels in and keep believing that things would work out. I could've easily sunk into a bad place, and at times I did, but I kept believing and stayed focused on being grateful for all that I had instead of looking at what I had lost. It's really easy to be positive when you're making money, but the challenge is to stay positive when things get hard. That is something that I was able to develop by staying focused on gratitude. Whenever I started to sink into a bad place, I would think about all the various ways I was a very fortunate person, and in time, it all paid off.

When I look back on my financial timeline, in 2010 (one of my lowest points), I was working at DSG for $8 an hour. By 2013, I was making $17 an hour and had a new car. By 2015, and once I made up my mind that I was going to make money and focus on that, I made $120,000 a year. When I got fired from BCS, I went back to my poverty mentality for a while because that had been my programming for so long, but I had built enough awareness by that point that I knew I could bounce back. If I had dug myself out of the hole before, then I knew I could do it again. I learned after all these rough experiences that I had to focus on the positive and not on the fear of what this

circumstance was bringing. My fear was always based on the lack of money, so I had to be mindful of what I was thinking about and where I was putting my attention. Was I going to focus on fear and lack as I had done so many times before? Or was I going to focus on the fact that I had gone through this before, I was now stronger and more aware, and would get through it again?
I chose the latter.

JOB #44: BBJ PRODUCTIONS ~ PRODUCTION ASSISTANT

My friend and writing partner Eileen's day job was working as an event producer. Events are fun to attend, but they aren't fun to work. At least that's my opinion, and probably thousands of other people who have worked events. The events this company would produce were for some very high-profile clients, including celebrities, art collectors, museums, billionaires, and more. When I needed to make extra money, Eileen invited me to work on a couple of events as one of the many production assistants to help with anything and everything, from setting up table linens to running out in a mad dash to pick up donuts that were being served as a wedding cake.

As a PA, you need to be prepared to do anything at any time, but other than that, it's a lot of hanging around. The nice thing about these events, though, was that they were high-end, and since L.A. weather allows for year-round, outdoor events and they were usually in cool locations, I didn't mind working these jobs. Plus, I was with Eileen, so that was fun too.

While working these events, I got to see James Taylor play in someone's backyard, and I worked a party for Max Martin, who is one of the biggest pop songwriters ever (and a nice guy). I also steamed the wrinkles out of Rod Stewart's stage clothes in his trailer before he performed for a private event. All good experiences. I honestly can't say anything negative about this one, aside from having to wear a uniform of a white polo shirt and *khaki* pants!

JOB #45: AUTISM ACCREDITATION AGENCY ~ INSIDE SALES REP

After the two freelance recycling jobs had failed, I was job hunting again for what felt like the nine hundredth time in my life, but there I was sending out resumes for a variety of sales positions. I didn't want to stay in the recycling business after having three bad experiences in a row, but it's not always easy to transition to a different industry in a competitive market like L.A.

After a few months of sending out resumes and doing phone interviews that went nowhere, I got a call from a young woman who was looking for an inside sales rep and said she was very impressed with my resume. That was a relief because there is so much frustration when you know you're perfect for a certain job, you send your resume, and hear nothing. Not to mention sending resume after resume for jobs I didn't even want but sent them anyway because I had the experience, or the job had a decent salary, or some other reason. I think it's unlikely that you'll enjoy your job if the motivation is just for the money or because you know you can do it, but if you took a poll on how many people have their jobs for one or both of those reasons, that might explain why so many people are unhappy at work.

I didn't want to do inside sales because I liked the freedom of outside sales better, but at this point, I again wasn't in a position to be picky, and I was happy for the possible gig. The bonus was that the office was in the WeWork building about a mile from my apartment on the corner of Hollywood Boulevard and LaBrea Avenue, and a short commute in this city is worth money. The WeWork building is directly across the street from the building I worked in for Bozo.

Once I was hired, there was a fairly steep learning curve because my job was to get these organizations to pay a fee that would put them through a process and potentially earn them an accreditation stating that they were operating with proper standards for autism care. Apparently, there has been quite a bit of fraud within this industry because the government funds the agencies who provide care for autism, but since it's a relatively new funding program, there aren't any watch dog organizations to check on where and how the money is spent, so people took advantage.

The young woman who started the company (we'll call her Susan) was a very smart, well-intentioned woman who was doing a great thing for the autistic community and was very knowledgeable about her industry. Once she hired me, she set up a phone call with a woman named Cathy, who was already doing sales for her remotely and living in Hawaii. Cathy knew the industry well because she had an autistic son and had dealt with these organizations for years and knew all the ins and outs as well as the terminology. When I had the phone call with Cathy, she told me how much she hated sales and thought that Susan was doing a lot of things wrong, but she believed in the company, so she stayed. What I didn't know at first was that Cathy had threatened to quit, and that is when Susan decided to start looking for someone new. Susan told me up front that Cathy was difficult, but she tolerated her because she was bringing in business. It was very strange to be in the middle of two people who seemingly didn't like working together but were doing it for a greater cause.

I started learning about autism and what the organizations provided and were supposed to provide for the autistic community. While doing research, I found it very interesting that in the nineties, autism was roughly one in twenty-five hundred. But thirty years later, it's one in fifty-four.

As I started to learn and understand my sales pitch, I asked Susan how she would be dividing the territories between Cathy and me. At this point, Cathy was calling on every state in the country, but now that I was added as a sales rep, it only made sense to split the states up so that we weren't stepping on each other's toes. Susan hadn't thought of this as a necessity until I started getting a few sales.

Suddenly Cathy became very territorial, literally.

When Susan started to divide the states, Cathy started telling her which states she wanted. She knew which states got the most federal funding, making them more likely to be a good prospect, so she was cherry picking. I was just struggling to gain confidence in what I was talking about and selling and doing my best to close sales. Two people that Susan had working for her—one as a project manager and the other in marketing—both made it clear that Cathy was difficult, caused problems, and was often rudely confrontational with people, including Susan. So why would you keep someone who caused so many problems?

Money, of course.

At first, I was hoping to learn from Cathy, but she started doing dirty things like calling on some of the organizations where I was gaining traction. When I brought this up to Susan, she tried to brush it off or make excuses for Cathy, and I had to explain to her that in sales, this was not okay. Susan was in her twenties and was new to running a company. She didn't understand certain things about sales. All sales reps know the importance of having territories. Otherwise, it becomes a free-for-all and there are unscrupulous sales reps who will snake into other reps territories, like what "Cunty Cathy" was doing.

As this continued with Cathy, I started to lose my patience and called her out on it directly, but in a professional way. Cathy got defensive and complained to Susan, who liked to keep things peaceful. Susan didn't appreciate that I called her out, and I again explained that what Cathy was doing was unfair and it undermined my ability to succeed at this job.

One thing working in my favor was that Susan started sending me to conferences because not only did Cathy live in Hawaii—so it was more expensive to send her anywhere—but she also could be a little abrasive to people. Susan liked me to represent, and I enjoyed the traveling. It also helped close sales when I got to meet people in person. However, the more sales I got, the dirtier Cathy's tactics became and I pointed this out. But for Susan, I was becoming a problem by mentioning it. At one point, Susan told me she hired me because she thought I could "handle Cathy" and I told her that I shouldn't have to "handle" anyone. I don't think you should hire someone because an employee threatens to quit and then keep them with the hopes that the new person can "handle" them. I was hired as a sales rep, not a babysitter. Also, after I had a few consecutive bad experiences in my other sales positions, I had a very low tolerance for this drama and sales in general. All I wanted was the opportunity to do a good job and make money without someone directly undermining me.

Susan's next solution to all of this was to hire a conflict resolution company, which was run by her aunt. I agreed to it because I was trying to show my willingness to be a team player and keep my job. But conflict resolution was not what was needed, and Cathy refused to do it anyway. I understood that Cathy was the money maker, but I didn't feel like I was being given a fair shot. By then, I had been working here for almost six months, and I could tell things were heading south. I had closed some sales, and I knew in time, I could do more, but the whole situation was really bumming me out. I wasn't being given the chance to succeed, so in the end, Susan and I both agreed it wasn't a good fit. I left in an amicable way, but I don't believe either one of us was unhappy about my departure, especially Cunty Cathy.

JOB #46: UBER/LYFT ~ DRIVER

I will start by saying that I wanted nothing less in life than to be an Uber or Lyft driver. Having driven on the mean streets and freeways of Los Angeles for over thirty years, I knew how absolutely awful it would be having a job that put you in the middle of that nightmare as a full-time job. Unless you're living under a rock, you've heard of L.A. traffic; it's almost as famous as the city itself. It's unbearable, and it has gotten worse every year that I have lived here. However, the appealing part of being a driver was the flexibility, and of course, not having a boss. More importantly, I had no choice. I was sending out resumes as always, but I had bills that weren't waiting until I found my next job, so a rideshare driver I became.

I *hated* it!

For starters, I didn't fully understand the platform because it takes some time to really grasp it and learn how and when to make the most money, and that was stressful. Other things that made it awful were things like the GPS not taking you exactly where you were supposed to go for the pick-up, or the person not being in the right place, or the customer having you waiting in an area that wasn't convenient, or pissing off other drivers, or someone getting in your car who smells bad. What made it worse was that you got paid on distance and not time, so you could get stuck in traffic and make shitty money on a ride that wasn't far but took an hour to complete. I believe on any rideshare platform, drivers should get paid on time, not distance (like a cab), especially when it takes you an hour to get to Los Angeles from Los Angeles!

I started with Lyft but eventually signed up for Uber too and learned how to maximize both platforms so that I could make enough money to live on. Despite my complaints, there were aspects of the job I enjoyed. My two favorite things about being a driver were seeing parts of the city that I had never seen before and having incredible conversations with people that I would only meet once in my life.

Los Angeles is a sprawling city, and in all my years of living here, there is still so much of it that I haven't seen and definitely would not have seen if it weren't for being a rideshare driver. L.A. is also very diverse in a variety of ways. The architecture is interesting because you can have a modern house right next to a Spanish-style house, right next to a craftsman house, right next to an art deco house, and so on. I would have the opportunity to drive into parts of the hood, which is spread all over the city in various areas, and I would get a glimpse into the city's history. There are amazing Victorian-style homes around USC that are beautiful, but you would never walk around there alone at night. There is also tons of Mexican culture and influence, which I love. Downtown L.A. has some very cool, historical structures that are now encapsulated by homeless encampments, and it's unbelievable to see. I drove a passenger who was a successful tech guy from India who told me he saw things in L.A. that he saw growing up in India and that he never would have believed he would see in the U.S. But then I would get a ride out to Malibu and be driving up the Pacific Coast Highway along the beaches. I would be in awe of what a beautiful city I live in when just an hour before I was in the dregs of the city, where it looked like a Third World country.

Then there were the conversations. People will sometimes confess things to you as a driver and I think it's because there's something safe in knowing you will never see them again and no one will have to know.

For example, I picked a guy up at a Ralph's supermarket in Compton one day. He had several bags, so I popped the trunk, he loaded his groceries, and then got into the back seat of my car. He was a friendly guy, so we started chatting.

"Are you from L.A.?" I asked.

"Yes, born and raised," he said. "Just doing a little shopping for the family." He started to tell me about his wife and his little boy and mentioned that his parents were very religious.

Whenever people start opening up, I usually just listen and try to give them the occasional "Yeah, I understand" or "I know what you mean" kind of response. I think everyone has a story, and I'm always curious once they start talking.

"I'm having kind of a rough day," he said.

"I'm sorry to hear that. Why is your day rough?"

He proceeded to tell me that he was on the suicide hotline the night before because he recently realized he was gay and didn't know what to do about it. Naturally, I was shocked to hear that and immediately started trying to convince him that being gay was okay, his life was valuable, and it was not worth ending it. I said, "You need to be here. There's nothing wrong with being gay and it doesn't matter what anyone in your family thinks. You have a son that needs you, and you need to be here for him."

"My biggest fear is that my family and wife are gonna disown me if I tell them," he said. He also told me I was the only person who knew this about him because he hadn't come out to anyone yet and was only realizing this about himself recently. I was so sad listening to this young man who was considering taking his life over something he couldn't hide anymore. What a horrible problem to have.

I continued to tell him that everything would be okay if he was honest about who he was and true to himself, but suicide was definitely the wrong choice. When I got to his house to drop him off, I helped him unload his bags out of the trunk and said, "Be brave, and everything will be okay." We instinctively hugged each other. It was a moment I'll never forget because I'd like to think that my words helped him that day. He thanked me, and as I drove off, I started to cry a little bit, knowing how tormented he must feel to have considered such a thing and think that was the only way out. I wish I knew how things turned out for him.

There was another ride I gave to a young woman who I picked up around Cedar Sinai Hospital. She got into the front seat. I never minded when a woman got into the front seat, but I can't say the same for when a man would get into the front seat without asking. The young woman and I started an easy conversation about how she was from somewhere in the Midwest and how she wasn't having an easy time in L.A. She was having relationship problems with a guy, and she unexpectedly and unwantedly got pregnant. Of course, I was as sympathetic as I could be to what sounded like a horrible situation to be in. She told me that she was planning on having an abortion but decided not to, and I had just picked her up from her first doctor's appointment. I told her I was happy she made that decision because *she* felt that was the right thing to do, and she said she knew it would be difficult, but she was excited about the baby. I was surprised how open she was but sometimes it helps to talk to someone who doesn't know you because if they judge or have an opinion, who cares? I think she opened up because she felt comfortable. It makes me feel good that strangers have felt like I was trustworthy enough in some way to open up to.

Naturally, there were very unpleasant experiences as well. People aren't always respectful of being in someone else's car. Some idiot spilled a milkshake in the back seat one time, and other people would eat and leave crumbs everywhere, which used to piss me off because I tried to keep my car clean for my passengers.

I picked up a creep once early morning one day in some weird area outside of downtown L.A. I only drove during the day. I was always on high alert when someone looked like they could be potentially dangerous or harmful, and when that happened, I would immediately strike up a conversation so I could find out just how creepy they were. He kind of had a gang member vibe.

"Good morning," I said as our eyes met in the

rearview mirror. He totally had the creep stare going.

He kind of mumbled "good morning" back.

He wouldn't look away from the mirror, so I started talking to him. "Did you grow up in L.A.?"

"Yeah."

"What part of the city?"

"Boyle Heights." Then he asked me if I liked to get high. I said once in a while. He said, "You want to pull over and get high."

I smiled and said, "I don't think that's a good idea since I'm driving."

And he just stared at me. I was getting creeped out for sure, but just then, thankfully, a new ride came though because it was a "pool" ride where you pick up more than one passenger so they pay less for the ride. I normally hated pool rides but was glad in this case. As soon as the new passenger got in, he shut up, and since he was the second of three passengers to get out of the car, I didn't have to be alone with him again.

Needless to say, some days were better than others.

Besides the interesting daily experiences I was having, driving also inspired me and my friend Chris, a fellow driver, to write a script for a TV show about rideshare driving, which you may or may not see on TV one of these days. I kept believing that one of our projects would eventually get picked up and/or that a better job would come along. Finally, it did.

JOB #47: L.A. STAR STORAGE ~ CUSTOMER SERVICE MANAGER

My sister, Kris, who was working in sales, went to visit a customer one day at a storage facility who asked her if she could refer anyone for a customer service position they had open. She thought of me right away, referred me to James (the owner), and the next day I called him, and we set up an interview for the following day.

I have to say that my sister was right when she was described the place to me as "so cool." This was not just any storage facility; this was the Fort Knox of storage! It was extremely high-tech, unbelievably safe and secure, and very state-of-the-art! There were cameras everywhere, and codes and fingerprints were needed to get into the storage areas beyond the garage. All of the storage rooms were temperature and humidity controlled with the perfect conditions for preserving film, tape, photographs, and other items that are worth keeping in the best condition possible. This company housed the master films and recordings of everyone from world famous directors to some of the top names in hip hop, as well as famous musicians and cultural icons. It was an unbelievable collection that you couldn't possibly put a value on.

When I interviewed with James, I immediately liked him because he seemed very nice and had a pleasant and friendly demeanor. I also met two of the men he employed: the CCO, Bart, who worked there for thirty years, and the CTO, Benjamin, who worked there for five years.

This was the whole team for the most part, aside from

James's wife Julia, who worked remotely, and the freelance archivist, Jack. After the interview, James told me to come in the next day and get started, and we would see how the first week went. Naturally, it went well and we both agreed this would be a good fit.

This job came along at the right time and was perfect for me! It was close to home and low stress. I was there to provide the kind of customer service that clients of this type of high-end facility would expect. But not many people came in on a regular basis. There were days that no clients came in at all, so it did get boring. With all the cameras around, there were usually eyes on me, but that was the only major downside because other than that, I was trusted to do my job without any kind of stress or pressure. I felt like the universe had delivered this gift to me almost as a way to make up for all the other shitty jobs and shitty bosses I had had up until then. Granted, my salary was less than what I had been making in sales, but it was a tradeoff for the lack of pressure and to be working for someone who I liked. Not to mention, that my driving days for Uber could come to an end, which was a huge relief, and I was able to get health insurance again. Everything was going great for about a year, and then…

COVID!

Once COVID hit and we were all on lockdown, James would ask me to go in on occasion and make sure everything was kept the way he liked it. I'm pretty sure I wasn't supposed to be doing that based on the strict "stay at home" order, but I did it anyway. Not many clients were coming in, but I was still going in once a week or so to collect mail or just tidy up when necessary. And just when I thought things couldn't get any better, they did.

One day, I happened to be at the facility at the same time as the CTO, Benjamin, who was a computer nerd and known to be very abrasive at times. Because there was no one else in the building, I didn't have a mask on and he freaked out. He made such a stink about it to James that James told me he wanted me to wear a mask even when I was alone in the building. I explained to him that the mask made it really hard for me to breathe, and I would wear it when necessary, and I was happy to wear it around people, but I couldn't wear it when I was alone. He kept insisting on it, and I kept pushing back by telling him that it was very uncomfortable and unnecessary. After a few minutes of my explanation, he settled on, "I'm sure you'll come around." I walked out of his office, angry, and drove home.

The reason I was angry was because I was the only person who was coming in full time. Bart continued to work from home, and Benjamin only came in when he had to work on a technology issue, but I was there daily from nine a.m. to six p.m. Now the guy who came in at his convenience was demanding that I wear a mask even when I was alone? That didn't sit right with me. The next day, I texted James and said I was taking a personal day.

Maybe he thought I was going to quit, but when I came in the following day, he pulled me aside and said, "I don't want to lose you. Why don't you work from home until all this blows over."

Work from home? I said, "Who will take care of things?"

"We'll find someone." Well, it turns out the CTO nerd wanted his stepson to have a job, so they had him fill in for me. Meanwhile, I couldn't believe my good fortune. There wasn't much for me to do from home considering my job was mostly customer service, so I was essentially getting paid to stay home, and what came out of that? This book, for starters. I had some free time on my hands and was able to work on my creative projects, which always makes me happy.

Those were some of the good things that came out of my working from home situation, but then the "party" was over, and I had to go back to work full time. It was rough! I know I am not alone when it comes to those of us who went from working at home for many months had to go back to our jobs and experience the misery that came with that. In fact, I was so unhappy after having all that freedom that my attitude about the job started to change. I started to almost hate going to work, but at this point, I had enough awareness to recognize that the job hadn't changed; my feelings about it did. I realized that because I remembered how happy I was when I got the job, and now I wasn't enjoying it anymore. What changed? My freedom was gone, and I was back to being watched all the time. I was still the only person working on site full time, which made me feel resentful, so I knew that I had to change my attitude or I was in trouble.

I kept struggling to feel good at work, so I came up with a plan as to how I could change my attitude: I would draw upon the knowledge and experience of those who I knew could help me. Every day, while doing my opening duties, I would put in headphones and listen to various types of motivational people. I would listen to podcasts or people on YouTube who taught about attitude, how our thoughts create our feelings, and how those two things create our circumstances. Just more of what I had now been studying for years, but now more diligently and focused. For months, I listened every day, and I started to feel better about the job. I practiced gratitude because I had been in so many worse situations, like being unemployed or having a terrible boss, so I made sure I focused on only what was good about the job, and it worked. I still had moments of negativity but would quickly catch myself and correct my thinking back to something positive.

This is something I would recommend for anyone who doesn't like their job. Just find one thing that's good about your job, whether it's an easy commute, good benefits, likeable coworkers, or something else, and just stay focused on that. It helps!

Sometime in March 2022, my friend Tom and I decided we had to go see the Rolling Stones concert in London, so we planned a two-week trip around it. James encouraged me to go and gave me the time off for the trip. When I got back, I had gotten COVID, so James told me to stay home until I tested negative. I was able to go back to work the following week, and the first day I was back, in the later part of the day, James told me to come to his office, and he let me know that his wife, Julia was with him. I thought, *Oh, it will be nice to see Julia; I haven't seen her in a while.*

When I got to the office, we said our hellos, and I sat

down on the couch, and James said, "Well, we're letting you go."

Considering there was nothing wrong as far as I knew, this came as a shock. James was always nice to me, and we never had any issues. Naturally, I asked why, and he said, "You know there have been communication problems." He was referring to a few former incidents when I mentioned that Bart hadn't responded on more than one occasion when I texted him about something, but I didn't think it was that big a deal.

"But I wasn't the one with the problem," I said. I think he was just using that as an excuse because I also think Ben, the CTO, wanted his stepson to have a permanent job. For some reason, Ben had a lot of influence with James.

They gave me severance pay, and I sat there while he and Julia told me that the severance was contingent on me signing an NDA, essentially once again taking hush money. I stood up and said, "Well, I think everything happens for a reason, so I'm sure something good will come out of this." They both looked surprised by my calm statement and demeanor. As I was walking out the door, Julia said, "But we really like you."

Funny way of showing it.

To this day, I'm not sure of the true motivation for letting me go, but Jack, the archivist who I am good friends with and has worked there for several years, agrees that it was Ben, the CTO, who really wanted me out. However, I saw it as a blessing in disguise because after I came back after COVID, I realized this job was not fulfilling, anymore. Not that it was ever truly fulfilling but I was satisfied with it for a while and would have stayed for a while longer until I realized it was a dead-end job, there was no upward movement available, and I was bored too often. Besides that, I wanted to make more money and wanted more freedom than the nine-to-five grind and being watched all the time. I really wanted a different situation, and I think the universe works that way sometimes. I asked for it without even directly asking for it and got something much better.

JOB #48: JIZZ-OFF! ~ OWNER

This didn't start out as a job, but it became one because when you start a company, you have a job!

While I was working from home at the storage facility and a few months after COVID hit, Eileen and I got together and were trying to come up with a way to help people and capitalize off the circumstances at the same time. So we invented a hand sanitizer. We came up with the name for it during a weekend trip to Palm Springs three years before, when I let my friends know that I had wiped all the jizz off of everything in the hotel room with disinfectant wipes. I'm sure you've heard the reports about all the semen they find in hotel rooms; it's on everything from light switches to the TV remote. I always wipe everything down in hotels with sanitizing wipes. We joked that weekend about a product called "Jizz off."

Cut to 2020, and our hand sanitizer, Jizz-Off! became a real product! We were referring to jizz as "the new germs," meaning that jizz was the new term for *all* germs. Everyone loved the idea. I won't bore you with the details of all that was involved in creating the product, but it definitely became a job. In addition to creating the actual hand sanitizer, we had to create a logo, get a website developed, figure out methods for payment, start an LLC, get insurance, and a lot of other details that you don't anticipate when you're in the creative mode. The business side isn't the fun part.

I asked Jamie Kennedy if he wanted to be a partner because I knew he would love it, which he did. It was an excellent product, and everyone got a kick out of it. It was a seventy-five percent alcohol liquid sanitizer with an added essential oil that made it smell great and kept your hands from drying out. We had a great logo and solid branding. In fact, we were asked to be a sponsor at the Miami Beach Gay Pride Parade that year. We had our product in some stores due to my sales calls and some of Jamie's connections. He was also selling it at his comedy shows, and we had some decent promotion on some podcasts thanks to Jamie.

Unfortunately, we hit the market about six months too late. By the time we got Jizz-Off! up and off the ground, everyone had already over-bought hand sanitizer, not to mention toilet paper. How could we forget that? I had a lot of people tell me if we had it on the market sooner, we would have sold out, so it was an issue of bad timing. We kept it going for two years and closed the business down in 2022. But I own the trademark, so don't be surprised if you see another Jizz-Off! product on the market some day!

Working on Jizz-Off! also contributed to feeling relieved when I was fired from the storage facility. I knew I had the capability to run a business, do sales, marketing, writing, and everything else, and I wasn't even coming close to my potential working there, including financially.

JOB #49: AMERICAN CHEMICAL SUPPLY ~ OUTSIDE SALES REP

Interestingly enough, a few weeks before I got fired from L.A. Star Storage, my sister Kris, who had moved back to the East Coast, said to me one day, "I wish you could take over my L.A. territory." Kris had built a very successful career in industrial chemical sales over the last five years she lived in L.A. and continued to service the territory by coming out to L.A. every six months or so. But she didn't feel like she could service her accounts the way she wanted because she wasn't living locally anymore.

After my conversation with James and Julia, I got into my car, and as I drove out of the parking lot, I called Kris and said, "I think I can take over your territory." Of course, when I told her they fired me, she was shocked because there was no indication that there was a problem. But something in me knew that this was for the best and this wasn't a random thing that was happening. I wanted more freedom in my job, and I wanted more money, and I knew somehow; I had manifested this! It was the first time I had gotten fired and didn't feel fear. I *knew* that it was a good thing!

Kris immediately called the owners of the chemical company and posed the idea of hiring me for the L.A. territory, and they thought this was a great idea. Within one month of getting the boot from L.A. Star Storage, I was officially hired by American Chemical Supply, where I would have the freedom that I craved, and the sky was the limit when it came to what I could earn!

Within one year of getting hired at ACS, my life was completely different, and in a great way. I knew I had "created" this new situation that had all the elements I had been working on manifesting, which were unlimited financial potential, freedom, and enjoying the job itself. Within a year and a half, I won a sales contest and expanded my territory by seventy-eight percent, and was making more money that I ever would have made at the storage place.

Once again, I was able to achieve it through the power of focus, mental discipline, self-awareness, and consistently paying attention to my thoughts and feelings. I know for a fact that these mental attributes can create a better life; it's just learning how to do it. I also became a better person in the process. I've learned more patience, I've become a more positive person, and I've been humbled.

I also learned over the years that no matter what your job is, you should appreciate it because it's serving a purpose, even if it's not your dream job. You're never stuck, even if it feels that way, and so much of success or failure has to do with your thoughts and attitude. It's not your boss, it's not your coworkers; it's always about you and your perception of your situation. You have the choice to show up every day with a good attitude or a bad one, and you have the power to change it if you want. For many years, I went to my day job with a bad attitude, and that created years of hardship and struggle. I didn't realize that at the time, but it's a lesson I hope to pass on. We are also living in a time where so much information and opportunity is available to us, and we have the ability to create the life we want if we learn how.

For me, my true fulfillment has always come from creativity and self-expression. If you're a creative person, it's definitely a bonus to have a day job you enjoy. I think feeling fulfilled in your work is what everyone wants but something that a lot of people are missing. Even with a day job that I succeeded and excelled at, I never stopped pursuing my dreams, and although fifty jobs would have been a nicer, rounder number to end on than forty-nine, I officially cut myself off here because I only can see one thing can happening:

My dreams become reality.

And my dreams as this point in my life are to write, perform when I can, hopefully help a few people by writing about the lessons I've learned, and maybe make the world just a little bit better.

JOB #50 ~ CELESTE DONOHUE

At this point in my life, my full-time job is ME! That requires working on myself daily to become more self-aware, happier, and healthier both physically and mentally. Because of that, this story has a very happy ending because after putting all of my trials and tribulations into writing, I was offered a publishing contract, and because of that, you are reading this book. Let's face it, everyone loves a happy ending!

When I started to write this book, my intention was to entertain people with the various stories of all of the jobs I've had, but as I got deeper into writing, I realized that there was a lot that I could pass on to others about lessons I've learned—mostly the hard way—and hopefully help others avoid some costly mistakes I've made along the way.

As such, here are my Top Ten lessons learned:

1.   YOUR ATTITUDE IS EVERYTHING.

Your attitude about your job will determine so much about your life because we spend a lot of time at our jobs. If you hate your job and you think about how much you hate it or talk about how much you hate it, or complain about it all the time, you are your own problem. You always have a choice: quit or change your attitude about it because no matter what job you have, if you have a bad attitude toward it, you are going to suffer in some way. Trust me, I am an expert on this!

2. DON'T BE AFRAID OF YOUR BOSS AND KNOW YOUR RIGHTS.

I've noticed that many people are afraid of their bosses just because they provide a paycheck, and I'd love for them to realize that they need you more than you need them. We are living in a time where working for yourself has never been easier, if you learn the skills. And bad bosses are just people who need therapy. No need to fear them.

Also, if you feel you are being treated unfairly in some way, educate yourself on your rights as an employee. If I didn't bother to find out my rights in the workplace, I would have gotten screwed over more than once without getting the money that was owed to me.

If you are an employer, listen up: The company is only as good as its employees. If you want an employee to do a good job, then treat them well. Be nice to them, care about them, be generous to them, treat them with respect, and you will get the best out of them. Otherwise, you will have employees who become resentful, apathetic, or insubordinate.

3. THERE IS AT LEAST ONE ASSHOLE AT EVERY JOB.

I actually think this is a universal law. In many cases, it's the boss, and I've had several of those, but it can also be coworkers who are just assholes for a wide variety of reasons. Even at the jobs I've had with just a few people, still at least one of them was an asshole. Who knows? Maybe some of the people I've worked with would say I was the asshole, and if you don't think there is an asshole at your job, maybe it's you.

4. THE AMERICAN WORK MODEL SUCKS.

Many Americans work the traditional nine to six, five days a week. It used to be nine to five, but employers decided they wanted a full forty hours out of their employees, so they stopped paying for an hour lunch break…and that's gross and greedy. Studies have shown that people aren't even that productive after five hours.

One week vacation out of fifty-two weeks in a year just because you haven't spent years at the job? That's ridiculous and unhealthy. One month of vacation per year is reasonable. We should use Europe's model. European Union legislation mandates that all twenty-seven member states must *by law* grant all employees a minimum of four weeks of paid vacation. Every employee is also entitled to twelve paid public holidays. America should take note.

5. THERE IS NO SUCH THING AS JOB SECURITY.

I have been fired more than once for no apparent reason. We've all heard stories of people who loyally went to the same job for thirty years, only to get fired without notice. Believe in yourself and believe that there is always a better opportunity if you look for it. Also, these days you can create your own opportunities. Look at all the people on the internet who have gained complete financial freedom and autonomy because they learned how to sell their skills (or something else) online.

6. DON'T YELL AT YOUR BOSS.

It turns out that yelling at your boss will get you fired. Yes, I know a lot of them deserve to be yelled at, but you'll never win in that situation. Learn a healthy way of communicating and realize that if they treat their employees with too much control or power, they are very insecure, and you should try to feel compassion for them because people like that aren't happy. And don't take it personally. I used to take everything personally, and it's never really about you; it's about them. But if you're reacting to them, you probably have some issues you could work on too because we all do.

7. THE PEOPLE AROUND YOU MATTER.

Regarding all the performing I've done, it's important to mention that at times when I felt doubtful about my talents or felt like giving up, I was fortunate enough to have people along the way who believed in me and encouraged me. I don't know if I would have kept going if there weren't other people, besides myself, who believed in me. Whether it was as a dancer, singer, comedian, or writer, there have always been people along the way that just said, "Keep doing what you're doing and keep on keepin' on." So, I did. And I haven't stopped.

8. FOCUS ON THE GOOD.

If you don't like your job, just pick one thing about it that's good and focus on that. Maybe you get to work from home, or you get great benefits, or they have great snacks at your job, or you like your coworkers. Just focus on the good! You can always find at least one thing. Also, when you're not working, do things that make you feel good. For me, my artistic pursuits provided some relief and made me feel happy. I eventually learned not to focus on the lack of what I had but on all the good that I had because life wasn't always awful. Despite my ongoing financial struggle and being in and out of jobs, I've had a lot of fun too. I met great people at every job, some of whom I am still friends with, performed in venues all across L.A., and experienced things you could only experience in this city. Not to mention all the skills I developed over the years from having all these jobs. So, find the good and focus on that.

9. LEARN ABOUT YOUR SUBCONSCIOUS PROGRAMMING.

If you don't like your job or don't feel fulfilled in your job, consider learning more about the programming that happens when we're young, and consider examining what messages you got about work, expectations, making money, and things like that. When I was young, I was taught that you have to work hard for money, and then watched my father work himself into two open heart surgeries that were brought on by the stress of having his own business, so that solidified that belief. I was told that I'd never get a good job without a college education. For many years I couldn't get a job making over $15 an hour until I started to learn and understand my own programming because these were messages that I internalized without knowing it. It also took me a long time to realize my own worth, and I had to overcome self-limiting beliefs to do that. On a conscious level, I knew I had the skills and talent to make a lot of money, but on a subconscious level, I had conflicting beliefs. Learning about our subconscious mind and what's stored in there can be a game changer.

10. BE GRATEFUL.

Whether or not you like your job, be grateful for it because being out of work and having no means of income sucks. In the world we are living in, we need money to survive, but how much money we make and how we make it has a lot to do with our deeply ingrained beliefs. But if you want to change your life, your attitude, or your circumstances and conditions, start by feeling grateful for whatever you have and especially the things that money can't buy.

Lastly, I've had a huge personal transformation throughout my years in Hollywood, and one thing I know for sure is that success is only guaranteed as long as you don't give up. No one knows how much time we have on this earth, and life is too short to not pursue your dreams or at the very least, enjoy your life and what you do for work. I hope this story inspires you to do more of what you love and leave behind anything that crushes your soul because we are not put on the earth to go to a job we hate for years, pay our bills, and die with regrets. The only thing I regret is that I didn't learn these lessons sooner. Thank you for reading, and always remember this:

"You miss one hundred percent of the shots you don't take." – Wayne Gretsky

www.ingramcontent.com/pod-product-compliance
Lightning Source LLC
Chambersburg PA
CBHW060353080526
44583CB00012B/298